❧ THE ❧
FAMILY
GARDEN

THE
FAMILY
GARDEN

*A practical guide to creating a
safe and enjoyable garden*

CLARE BRADLEY

LORENZ BOOKS
LONDON • NEW YORK • SYDNEY • BATH

SYMBOLS

○ Prefers sun
◑ Prefers partial shade
● Prefers shade
❋ Tender
✳ Half-hardy
✿ Suitable for small gardens
✖ Poisonous

(where no hardiness symbol appears the plant is fully hardy)

First published in 1997 by Lorenz Books

English text © Anness Publishing Limited 1997
© text and special photography 1997
DuMont Buchverlag, Köln,
Federal Republic of Germany

Lorenz Books is an imprint of
Anness Publishing Limited
Hermes House, 88-89 Blackfriars Road
London SE1 8HA

This edition is distributed in Canada by
Raincoast Books Distribution Limited

ISBN 1 85967 274 4

Designed and edited by Anness Publishing Limited

PUBLISHER: Joanna Lorenz
SENIOR EDITOR: Clare Nicholson
DESIGNER: Nigel Partridge
PHOTOGRAPHER: Marie O'Hara
ILLUSTRATOR: Vana Haggerty

Printed and bound in Germany

1 3 5 7 9 10 9 8 6 4 2

CONTENTS

INTRODUCTION

It is perfectly possible to create a garden for the whole family to enjoy – a place of beauty, fragrance and colour of which you are proud, and a safe and exciting play area for children. If you are new to gardening and a first-time parent, then the value of your garden has probably just dawned on you; it is likely to become one of your most valuable allies. Before children arrive on the scene, we tend to be more mobile and the garden is often of secondary use. However, a baby makes us more home-bound, and immediate surroundings become far more important and precious.

While the outside world may seem threatening to your baby, a garden offers the possibility of creating a haven right on your doorstep, where your child can play with a measure of safety and experience all the good things the larger world

offers: sunshine, birds, animals, plants and any number of games. Children need space to play in – as much as is available. And if at the same time they can get out from under your feet and get some fresh air into their lungs, then surely it makes sense to plan a child-friendly garden for them to enjoy fully.

From the day your baby first crawls away from the safety of the play mat, your beautiful, relaxing garden becomes a jungle of possible dangers. Faced with the potential horrors, many parents resign themselves to containing small children in play pens and ruling older ones with a rod of iron. Alternatively, they might glumly give up altogether, coming to regard the garden as nothing more than a barren, muddy patch completely taken over by the children and filled only

LEFT: A large, uncluttered expanse of grass is invaluable for active games. A family lawn will never be an immaculate green sward, but regular care will ensure it survives the rough and tumble of children's games. A simple design makes the best possible use of available space and is particularly important in a small family garden.

OPPOSITE: If you can afford a wonderful garden feature such as this gazebo, it could serve as a Wendy house or private den for small children. When the children get older it can become a peaceful shelter for adults or a glorified garden shed.

with bicycles, climbing frames and a sandpit that is also (inevitably) a favourite with next door's cat. Thankfully, it does not have to be like this.

For the many parents who caught the gardening bug while still child-free, be assured that gardening does not have to stop once children arrive. Creating a child-friendly garden certainly does not mean that you have to turn your plot into an amusement park, but nor does it mean having a single play feature that you hope will keep youngsters amused for hours. The garden should suit everyone. It should be an attractive, relaxing place for you, as well as being a valuable outdoor room that is safe and fun for your children.

As the children grow and change, so should the garden. Safety is the main priority because toddlers need to be protected but, as they grow up and play becomes rougher, it is invariably the case that the garden requires protection from the children! With inventiveness and planning, you can anticipate these changes and make compromises that are not too painful. That way everyone is happy and you are still left with the beautiful, stylish garden you always wanted.

Children can grow bored easily, so it is important that there are plenty of things to do. A child-friendly garden may contain features such as paddling pools, sandpits, cycle tracks and wild areas, but this does not necessarily mean spending vast sums of money on manufactured playthings – many of these can easily be made from recycled or throw-away objects, and never forget that the world of the imagination often gives children the greatest pleasure. The garden can provide the perfect setting for a child's fantasy world; in the book *Alice in Wonderland*, Alice looks through the door and discovers "the loveliest garden you ever saw", and that is where her adventures began.

OPPOSITE: *It is essential that climbing equipment is robust and sturdy, whether it comes in kit form or is home-made. This large kit, though not cheap, will provide plenty of thrills for a group of children.*

RIGHT: *A delightful crooked house, complete with veranda and chimney, is built on stilts with a short stairway approaching it. Straight out of a nursery story, many an hour can be whiled away here in imaginative play.*

CHAPTER ONE

SAFE GARDENS

As well as being a safe place for playing and learning, the garden should be a haven of fantasy for your children and their friends. It can even be a place where they learn to look after themselves, and where you can safely instil a sense of trust in older children by encouraging them to look after the younger ones.

Children between the ages of two and five years, when they are extremely active but have little sense of danger, are most vulnerable to accidents. However, if parents are aware of the hazards, the risks can be greatly reduced.

Above: This shallow stream provides a great safe water feature for older children.

Opposite: A safe garden will bring peace of mind. Minor scrapes and scratches are part of garden life, but to prevent more serious accidents it is important to avoid hidden dangers and to have a large clear area for children to play in, avoiding accident "hot spots" such as steep steps, sharp corners, slippery surfaces and prickly plants.

STORING CHEMICALS AND TOOLS

Chemical products and tools are major causes of garden accidents, and their safe storage will be one of your first concerns. Many gardeners keep such items in a garden shed, in an outside cupboard or in a storage bin. Unfortunately, these often dark and out-of-sight places are magnets to children, being attractive as hiding places as well as exciting play areas for older children. It is vital, therefore, that any shed, cupboard or storage bin has a secure lock.

Some of the hazards of garden chemicals can be reduced if you remember the basic guidelines outlined below. Safety rules are also important for garden tools, especially as many

are made of steel or iron and have sharp blades, edges or points. If tripped over, stepped on, thrown or wildly swung about, such tools can be very dangerous. To avoid injuries to children, or damage to expensive tools, keep all garden implements neatly stored and locked away. When not in use, most tools can be hung from strong pegs or racks. Turn the rake and lawn mower so that the tines and blades are facing the wall. Hose pipes can be kept safely coiled on wall-mounted frames or cassette hose reels.

When tools are out in the garden, make sure that forks are always stuck in the ground when not actually in use, and that rakes are laid with their tines pointing downwards. Electric power tools, such as hedge cutters, can also be a danger. If possible, use them when children are not about.

Stakes, canes and poles for supporting plants are often used during summer months. As the plants grow, these can become hidden beneath the green stems and leaves, and their sharp ends forgotten. Cover all stakes and bamboo poles with rounded caps to prevent them from poking into eyes when you or your children bend over. And finally, remember that any unfamiliar object will be explored and played with.

STORING AND USING CHEMICALS

★ Never buy chemicals "just in case" you might need them at a later date.

★ Never change the original purpose of containers: for example, do not use a drinks bottle for chemicals.

★ Never remove or throw away labels attached to chemical products. If the label is lost or unclear, dispose of the product safely. Many councils have special facilities for the handling of unused garden chemicals; investigate whether such facilities exist before throwing chemicals into the rubbish bin.

★ Never keep made-up spray solutions to use later, but dispose of them carefully.

★ Always buy the appropriate chemical for the problem; read the label carefully and make sure that the chemical is the one you need.

★ Always follow the instructions for use on the product, including the "use by" date.

RIGHT: Tools with sharp prongs should be hung up out of reach of children, with the prongs facing the wall.

OPPOSITE: Jam jars are useful for capping the tops of larger stakes and binders.

BELOW: These bamboo sticks have been topped with a safety cap.

SAFE PLANTS

We often remember learning with morbid fascination as children that innocent-looking plants can be deadly poisonous. We are quite used to seeing many of them on a daily basis, but have we been dicing with death?

Although there are many plants in our gardens that would be harmful if eaten in large enough quantities, this does not mean that by growing them we are necessarily putting ourselves at risk – it is important to keep the potential danger of poisonous plants in perspective. Educating children is vital. The first lesson is not to eat any plant at all unless a responsible adult gives permission to do so. By the time children can talk, at the age of two-and-a-half to three years, they have usually understood this message, although the identification of potentially harmful plants comes much later.

EMERGENCY AID

If you suspect poisoning due to eating plants

It is advisable to have an emergency number ready to hand in case of poisoning. Keep it in a clear and obvious place.

★ Do not try to make the child sick.

★ Take him or her immediately to a doctor or to the accident-and-emergency department of a hospital, with a sample of the plant for identification.

★ Note the time of eating, and any symptoms (these may appear many hours later).

For skin or eye irritation caused by a plant

★ Wash the affected area with clean water.

★ If in doubt, seek medical advice. Remember to take a sample of the plant with you.

Be careful to set a good example to toddlers by avoiding picking and then eating plants, fruit or berries as you walk round, because they might get the wrong message. While children are small it is probably a good idea to grow vegetables and herbs in a separate patch, away from the rest of the garden, making an area for edible plants with clearly identified boundaries.

Some plants are mildly poisonous; others are deadly if eaten. The berry of a yew (*Taxus baccata*) has a succulent, bright-red fleshy aril (an appendage on the seed) that begs "eat me, eat me". The red flesh is harmless enough, but just one seed could prove fatal. Some plants can also cause serious skin reactions just by being handled. And some poisons can even be absorbed through the skin, so discourage children from playing with plants generally, particularly berries. Make sure that they always wash their hands after coming indoors, and teach them not to put their fingers in their mouths while playing in the garden.

ON YOUR GUARD!

Protect all your family by learning to recognise harmful plants. It is general practice among garden centres to label all potentially harmful plants so, before you buy, read the label carefully. Take stock of your garden, and your houseplants, and make a note of any plants that you know to be poisonous or irritants. If you are unsure about any plants, get them identified by an expert.

Once you have identified any hazardous plants, take action: warn your children about them, get rid of them, or transplant them to a less accessible area of the garden, such as the back of a border where children are unlikely to come into contact with them. Brightly coloured berries are particularly seductive to children. If you have berrying shrubs in a prominent position, it may be feasible to prune off all the flowers as they fade to prevent the berries from forming.

ABOVE: Small children need educating as to which plants are harmful as they are always putting things that they pick in the garden into their mouths.

Having taken these measures, do not just warn children about specific plants, but emphasise the main message: leave all plants alone. This should ensure their safety in your garden, and in others that they visit.

EFFECTS OF POISONOUS PLANTS

Nature often has its own way of dealing with mild toxicity. A slightly poisonous plant will usually cause diarrhoea or vomiting which, although unpleasant, actually stops poison from entering the system. And, in many cases, the poisonous plant has such an unpleasant taste that only a little can be eaten, so lessening the risk of greater harm. Plants that contain irritant sap can cause very serious reactions when they come into contact with the skin in bright, sunny weather. Symptoms may vary from redness and itching to severe blistering that lasts for several weeks, sometimes resulting in long-term skin discoloration. Rue (*Ruta graveolens*) is an example of a plant that can have such serious effects; this should not be grown in any garden where children play. If you have to handle plants that may have irritant sap, be sure to wear gloves and long sleeves, and try to work in the early evening or morning rather than in bright sunshine.

15

THE MOST COMMON HARMFUL PLANTS

This list of plants is a guide to the most common harmful plants. It includes houseplants and garden plants, some are dangerous because they are toxic and some because they are prickly. An ✖ sign indicates the most toxic entries.

Monkshood *(Aconitum napellus)* ✖
All parts of the plant contain poisons that can be fatal if eaten. Fortunately, fatalities are very rare because the plant

tastes so disgusting that very little is ever eaten. However, the poison is easily absorbed through the skin, so children may be endangered if they play with the flowers or foliage.

Cuckoo pint *(Arum italicum)* ✖
The berries are toxic if eaten, and their bright colour may prove attractive to children.

Deadly nightshade *(Atropa belladonna)* ✖
All parts of the plant can cause serious poisoning, and can be fatal even in small quantities. The berries are most likely to be eaten by children, who may perhaps mistake them for blackcurrants or elderberries.

Berberis *(Berberis)*
These are popular hedging plants but beware their dangerous spines. They are on the stems and leaf tips.

Cacti
Cacti are well known for their spines and needle-like hairs. Though attractive, they can be very dangerous.

Sedge *(Carex)*
The sedges are grass-like in appearance, but many species have sharp leaf margins that can cause very fine cuts.

Meadow saffron *(Colchicum autumnale)* ✖
All parts are highly poisonous – especially the flowers, corm and seeds – and have caused fatalities.

Lily-of-the-valley *(Convallaria majalis)* ✖
All parts – especially the seeds – are poisonous, but they do taste unpleasant, making it difficult to eat a large quantity.

LEFT: *Monkshood* (Aconitum napellus).

ABOVE: *Foxglove* (Digitalis purpurea).

Pampas grass *(Cortaderia)*
This specimen grass grows up to 3m (10ft) tall, and the long leaves have very sharp, tough edges. The plants often need tidying up in spring by removing the old leaves – be sure to wear a strong pair of gloves for this job.

Leyland cypress *(x Cupressocyparis leylandii)*
Inhalation of the smoke when this plant is burned, or having contact with the sap when pruning, can cause allergic skin rashes. If you are allergic to sticking plasters, you are likely to react to this plant.

Spurge laurel *(Daphne laureola)* ✖
All parts of the plant are toxic, and the berries might look attractive to children.

Dumb cane or Leopard lily *(Dieffenbachia)* ✖
If any of the plant is eaten, even in small quantities, it can make the tongue, mouth or throat swell up, interfering with breathing. Just touching the sap can cause a skin rash.

Foxglove *(Digitalis purpurea)* ✖
All parts can cause serious poisoning, even in small quantities, but fortunately the plant tastes extremely bitter and is likely to cause vomiting first, so serious cases are rare.

Golden barrel *(Echinocactus grusonii)*
Razor-sharp, long yellow spines are typical of the cactus family. These give a clear warning of the punishment on offer, but watch out for other cacti with smaller spines; they might not look as fierce but can be the devil to remove.

Spurge *(Euphorbia)* ✖
The white sap, or latex, can cause a burning sensation and skin rash, and if any of the plant were eaten it would cause burning and inflammation of the mouth.

California glory *(Fremontodendron)* ✖
The stems and leaves are covered with minute, hair-like growths that can cause skin irritation and itching. Some people are more sensitive than others, but avoid touching your eyes, nose or mouth after handling this plant.

Hyacinth *(Hyacinthus orientalis)* ✖
If you mistook this for an onion it might make you sick; if you are particularly sensitive it is possible to get a skin rash from handling the bulbs.

*ABOVE LEFT: Holly (*Ilex aquifolium*).*
ABOVE RIGHT: Laburnum.

Holly *(Ilex aquifolium)*

There are many different types of holly: some species have smooth leaves, others extremely spiny ones. The hedgehog holly (*I. aquifolium* 'Ferox') is very well-endowed in the spine department, being equipped with spines on the edges as well as the surfaces of its leaves.

Laburnum *(Laburnum)* ✖

All parts are poisonous, but the black seeds – contained in twisted pods – can be attractive to children. Fortunately, there have been few reported cases of poisoning in recent years, and vomiting usually lessens the risk of fatalities. The cultivar *Laburnum* x *watereri* 'Vossii' flowers just as well as the others, but, as it rarely sets seeds, is much safer.

Lantana *(Lantana camara)* ✖

All parts of the plant are toxic, and the unripe berries might prove attractive to children.

Lupin *(Lupinus)* ✖

The seeds and pods are poisonous, but would have to be eaten in large quantities to cause any real harm.

*RIGHT: Rue (*Ruta graveolens*).*

Daffodil *(Narcissus)* ✖

Children could mistake daffodils for onions because they are stored in the same way. After eating, the effects would be nausea, vomiting, stomach ache and diarrhoea, but daffodils will not cause severe illness. Just to be on the safe side, store daffodil bulbs out of the reach of children.

Bunny ears *(Opuntia microdasys)*

With a deceptively friendly name for a distinctly unpleasant character, the pads of this plant are covered with tufts of bristles. However, just one touch to see if they are sharp will leave you removing the tiny hairs for hours, if not days.

German primula *(Primula obconica)* ✖

This is one to look out for, as it can cause quite severe dermatitis. As the allergen is found mainly on the bracts surrounding the flowers, simply removing the dead flower heads by hand can cause a reaction.

Pyracantha *(Pyracantha)* ✖

Usually grown against a wall, the stems have sharp thorns that need handling with a thick pair of gloves. The berries are very brightly coloured and mildly poisonous.

Castor oil plant *(Ricinus communis)* ✖

All parts of the plant – especially the seeds – are highly poisonous, and can prove fatal. The seeds are quite a feature although they form only in long hot summers.

Rose *(Rosa)*

Roses may be armed with serious thorns which are capable of causing nasty scratches. However, there are many excellent thornless varieties of rose available.

Rue *(Ruta graveolens)* ✖

All parts of the plant can do serious damage, especially when they come into contact with skin during sunny weather. Severe burning and skin blisters can occur, which may last for weeks and leave the skin discoloured.

Umbrella tree *(Schefflera)* ✖

Contact with cut stems or leaves may cause a skin rash.

Winter cherry *(Solanum capsicastrum)* ✖

A popular winter houseplant, grown for its festive fruits, which turn from green through yellow to bright orange and might well attract the attention of children. The fruit is poisonous but not fatal.

*ABOVE: Yew (*Taxus baccata*).*

Woody nightshade *(Solanum dulcamara)* ✖

The berries of this plant are much less toxic than those of deadly nightshade (*Atropa belladonna*), but they can still cause sickness, diarrhoea and a sore throat.

Yew *(Taxus baccata)* ✖

All parts are toxic except the fleshy arils, or berry-like parts. Eating or even just chewing the seeds can be deadly.

Gorse *(Ulex europaeus)*

This well-known plant of the countryside, with its bright yellow, pea-like flowers, is densely spiny, as you will know if you have ever fallen into one.

Wisteria *(Wisteria)* ✖

All parts of this plant, across every species, are harmful, especially the seeds and pods.

Adam's needle *(Yucca filamentosa)*

Adam's needle is a very apt name because the leaves are stiff and needle-sharp. This plant is not good for the family garden because the leaves grow dangerously at about child height. An alternative spiky plant is the New Zealand cabbage palm (*Cordyline australis*), which has much softer leaves.

SAFE STRUCTURES AND SURFACES

When developing a garden structure, and before introducing any new feature or object into the garden, try to ensure that it is as safe, robust and, of course, as child-friendly as possible. You should take into account, too, how objects will change with age and whether they will stand the test of time.

One of the most important features in any garden where there are children is an open, all-weather space such as a terrace, patio or deck area. For the safety of young children, the area should be within sight of the house, so that they can easily be watched continuously. The material that you choose for surfacing this area will greatly affect its use and your comfort throughout the year. Lawn grasses are soft to play on and cool in hot sun but, if heavily used, they give way to summer dust and winter mud. Bark chippings, thickly laid and retained within a compound of logs, will soften falls and provide a good surface for games; they are now available in a variety of colours.

Paving stones, bricks or other hard surfacings are virtually immune from winter weather. However, rainwater will collect

and puddle on a flat surface, leading to the growth of slippery algae; to prevent this, have hard surfaces laid professionally and discuss the drainage "fall" across the area. Wooden decking will both allow rainwater to drain and be soft for children when they fall over, and, as it is raised off the ground surface, stays clean throughout the year. It is expensive but very stylish.

A safe and special feature of any flat surface such as a lawn or patio could be a maze, a labyrinth or even a hopscotch area marked out in a different-textured material. For the latter, use flat stones or pavers laid into a lawn, setting them lower than the level of the turf to avoid interfering with the mowing. On a hard patio surface, use paving with contrasting textures or patterns, which in itself will appeal to children who will construct all sorts of games around them. The game of hopscotch is thought to be based on a labyrinth, and also has links with ancient maze dances.

A sloping garden may require steps or terracing, but avoid any unexpected or sudden changes of level. Always build wide, shallow steps, which even in a small garden can be a feature. When making steps, it is important that all the increases in height are equal.

OPPOSITE: Paving stones provide a good surface for play all year round. This patio is well-positioned and has two shallow steps down on to the lawn.

RIGHT: If your garden has steep steps, encourage children to climb them with great care.

ABOVE: Bark chippings create the perfect surface for play areas because they are soft and hard-wearing.

Benches and garden seats provide welcome rest when you are playing with children in the garden. Beware of light-weight or flimsy furniture that could tip over when children climb on it, or splinter with age. Choose solid, heavy benches that stand firm, or fix wooden seats securely to the tops of low walls. Similarly, all ornaments and barbecue structures should be stable and fixed, to avoid being used as playthings. Finally, when you have checked for safety, sit back and pour yourself a long, cool drink.

SAFE WATER

Water and children are an all-too-easily fatal combination. This does not mean that the family gardener should be denied having both together, but the challenge is to incorporate water without risking young lives.

Water has many wonderful properties: bubbling and rushing, it can bring energy, movement and life into a garden;

ABOVE: A drain at one corner of a water channel means great fun can be had building a dam with sand to stop the water draining away. When the channel is empty it provides a decorative surrounding to the paved terrace.

LEFT: This is a water channel that runs around the three outside edges of a terraced area which is against a house. The water is turned on at the wall of the house and slowly fills the channel, creating a very shallow stream for children to play in.

whereas still, reflective surfaces encourage tranquillity and contemplation. With wetland habitats rapidly disappearing from our environment, garden ponds of all sizes have become an important network for many forms of wildlife. It is likely that the number of species visiting your garden will almost double if you add water. A pebble fountain will not encourage breeding frogs and toads, but it will provide a welcome watering spot for birds, all sorts of insects and, if you are lucky, maybe even a hedgehog.

LEFT: *Water adds interest to any garden. Wall fountains will delight all ages and are safe for young children.*

BELOW: *Although safe for young children, even this small amount of water could prove fatal to a toddler. To eliminate any risk, the pebbles should be placed on a metal grille separated from, and held above, the water reservoir.*

It is not surprising that water also acts as a magnet to children, providing an almost endless source of fascination. Unfortunately, the horrifying truth of the relationship between water and children is that a toddler can drown in just a few centimetres of water, and that there are many accidents of this kind every year. No pond, however shallow, is safe for small children. Luckily, it is not all doom and gloom because there is a simple answer to safe water: choose a design such as a pebble fountain, where the water is completely covered or filled with cobblestones, or a wall fountain which is situated high up out of reach.

SAFE WATER FEATURES

There are all sorts of attractive and imaginative water features available with hidden or buried water reservoirs, giving them all the virtues of moving water but none of the hazards, and making them completely safe. Water for this fountain is supplied by a small reservoir containing a submersible pump which recycles the water over a decorative covering, such as cobblestones. These water features take up very little space and, whereas a more conventional pool

RIGHT: Bubble fountains are simple and inexpensive to construct. A small submersible pump, a container and some pebbles are all the materials you need.

BELOW: A bright plastic toy-tidy can make an ideal first pond. It is large enough to accommodate a couple of small marginal plants and some tiny floating ferns.

requires full sunlight, they can be used in total shade – even under trees and hedges. They are also fairly simple to make yourself. Apart from the initial outlay for a submersible pump, a water feature can be constructed from cheap or recyclable materials, as in the design above using a plastic dustbin.

MAINTENANCE

During the winter months water can look rather dismal and pumps can be damaged by freezing conditions, so it is worthwhile emptying a small water feature at this time of

MAKING A BUBBLE FOUNTAIN

1 Using a saw, cut the dustbin in half horizontally. The bottom half will make the reservoir.

2 Dig a hole deep enough to sink the bottom half of the dustbin into the ground.

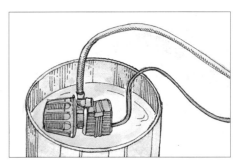

3 Fix 1.2m (4ft) of hose pipe to a small submersible pump, and place in the reservoir. Half-fill it with water.

4 Place the lid upside-down on top of the reservoir and feed the hose pipe up through the central hole. You may place a plant pot saucer on top, feeding the pipe through the central hole.

5 Cut the hose pipe off 2cm (¾in) proud. Make sure that the cable passes over the edge of the bin base and under the lid. Cover the lid with pebbles.

6 Get an electrician to connect the pump to an electric supply. If you have very young children, make sure that the pebbles are completely covered with water.

year and storing the pump in a frost-free place. In the spring, give it a good clean and you are ready to start all over again.

MINI-PONDS

When children are well beyond the toddling stage and are desperate for a pond of their own, a mini-pond could be the answer, especially where space is limited. They are easy to position close to the house: for example, on a patio in front of the kitchen window or even on a balcony. A stylish mini-pond is made from a wooden half-barrel, but you must soak this beforehand so that the wood swells and makes the barrel watertight. Any large container will do instead, as long as it is water- and weatherproof. A cheap version is a stacking plastic toy-tidy; children will love the bright colours.

A mini-pond is too small for fish, but will be a bonus for visiting thirsty birds. One or two small aquatic plants such as golden sedge (*Carex stricta* 'Bowles Golden') and a monkey flower (*Mimulus*) is all it needs, plus one or two oxygenating plants to keep the water fresh. Site the pond in a shady spot to keep down the water temperature in the summer.

MAKING EXISTING WATER FEATURES SAFE

Ponds can offer a wonderful opportunity for children to observe and enjoy aquatic creatures and plant life, and it would be a shame to deny them the experience. At the age of about three, youngsters begin to understand the concept of danger and start to heed warnings and instructions given to them, so you can begin relaxing a little. However, the risks

that ponds can present to the under-four age-group should never be under-estimated.

Children aged between one and two years suddenly acquire increased mobility, and at times they can move at a terrific rate. One minute they are at your feet and the next they have escaped, which means that they can get into difficulties unexpectedly quickly. However, even though movement can be speedy, stability and co-ordination are still touch-and-go, which leads to plenty of stumbles and difficulty in getting going again. Regaining footing in a slippery pond, or lifting a head from the water, can pose a problem for a toddler who has tumbled. Even when you have made sure that there is only safe water in your own garden, you must still be on your guard when visiting friends, relatives and neighbours who may have ponds, because that is where the vast majority of accidents happen.

Do not overlook hazards such as a water butt that does not have a secure cover. A child retrieving a stray ball could easily fall in, resulting in a serious accident.

KEEPING THE POND

If the pond is your pride and joy, and you want to share it with your children, the best way of protecting them from accidents is to fit a rigid wire mesh over the top. Ready-made mesh covers do not seem to exist, probably due to the wide variety of shapes and sizes of ponds. However, security-grille suppliers can cut meshing to size on request, although it is important that this material is heavy-duty and will not sag in the middle, as some types of wire (such as chicken wire) would probably do. As a temporary solution – for protecting visiting grandchildren, for example – a home-made grid built

LEFT: If your garden has a water feature that cannot be adapted, you must ensure that it is securely fenced off and fitted with a gate that cannot be opened by children.

Right: Toddlers are the age group that are most at risk from drowning in ponds. But this is also the age when a sandpit is popular. If you have a pond but are nervous about your children falling in, convert it into a temporary sandpit. This sandpit, which started out as a pond, would also make an excellent cold frame to protect delicate plants and seedlings when your children have grown out of building sandcastles. The slatted roof, which can be rolled up when the sandpit is in use, prevents cats getting into the sandpit.

from chicken wire and wooden slats would suffice, but make sure that it is tensioned and fixed securely. Strong wooden trellising could also be used as an alternative to mesh, although it is not as strong and, being bulkier, will not blend in naturally with the surroundings.

Fencing

Fencing off the pond is another option, but this is only a partial solution and can lead to a false sense of security. If the pond is fenced, a gate will be needed to provide access for maintenance, and gates can accidentally be left unlocked.

Gates

If you have a gate that leads to a water feature which is not safe for children, it should be fitted with a childproof catch and a strong spring to ensure that it shuts.

CHANGE OF USE

A pond that is a permanent feature of the garden could be emptied and adapted while children are small. The conversion could be to a sandpit, a flower bed, or even a bog garden. Alternatively, an attractive permanent cover could be made from wooden slatting to make a play surface for toys such as racing cars. It almost goes without saying, of course, that such a measure needs regular checking to ensure the continuing soundness of the wood.

WATER FOR PLAYING

A paddling pool brought out on a hot, summer's day is a brilliant way to provide water to play in in even the smallest gardens. While the children are using the pool, they should not be left unattended, and if it is not put away after use, it should be emptied completely.

SAFE GREENHOUSES AND CONSERVATORIES

Greenhouses and conservatories come in all shapes and sizes, so take time to choose the right structure for your needs. You may decide that a cupboard-like, wall-mounted or lean-to greenhouse, providing enough space for a grow-bag, some seed trays and even a crop of tomatoes, will suit you. On an even smaller scale, cloches in plastic or PVC are ideal for vegetables or individual tender plants.

If you need more space for growing purposes or relaxing in, then a greenhouse or conservatory is for you. With a

conservatory, there is strict legislation controlling the use of glass in construction, so seek professional advice. As a guide, for roofs and wall areas below waist level you must either use safety (toughened) glass, or a glass substitute such as twin-wall polycarbonate. As a bonus, these safety materials give increased protection against burglaries because they do not shatter. Greenhouses are not covered by such strict legislation, and horticultural glass is often thin and can break into dangerous shards. With children about, it would be wise to use either acrylic sheet or toughened glass, although the latter may be too thick to fit the glazing bars of many prefabricated greenhouses. Initially, both acrylic sheet and toughened glass will be more expensive than thin glass, but both will resist most misfired balls. Greenhouses with half-timbered sides are very attractive and, although they may not be as bright as, or have the growing space of all-glass structures, they are safer with small children around and are also more efficient to heat, reducing the fuel bill.

The areas surrounding a greenhouse should be kept tidy and free of hazards to prevent children from tripping or stumbling and possibly falling against the glass. Separate the play area from any greenhouse structure, either by distance or by placing free-standing trellis panels between the greenhouse and any paths, lawn or patio areas, or by planting shrubby plants as a shield. Use deciduous plants for this purpose, so that the bare stems do not have to compete for scarce winter light. Shrubs such as lilac, buddleia and deutzia can be pruned each year to remove as much or as little woody growth as is

LEFT: This greenhouse has been separated from the rest of the garden by a free-standing trellis. Grow deciduous climbing plants against it – they will cast welcome shade over the greenhouse in summer and let in all available light in winter. This screen also gives added protection when children are playing in the vicinity.

RIGHT: Although this vigorous climbing rose will help deflect the odd flying ball, this greenhouse is still quite exposed. You could protect the sides with a layer of strong netting.

BELOW: The half-timbered sides on this greenhouse provide good protection for toddlers.

needed to maintain the open structure. Among the shrubs, trellis panels could be positioned in vulnerable places where the glass is most exposed to ball games. Plant the trellis with deciduous climbers such as clematis varieties, or with open shrubs such as the slow-growing flowering quince (*Chaenomeles speciosa*).

For home-made or temporary structures such as a lean-to, cold frame or cloche, there are several other safe glass substitutes such as acrylic and PVC. Acrylic sheets 2.5mm (1/16 in) thick have good light transmission, can be drilled and cut (using a tenon saw and hand drill), and have a life expectancy of approximately eight years. PVC can be purchased in both light and heavy weights, and may be covered by a guarantee of up to ten years.

Wherever plants are growing and water is sloshed about, slippery surfaces can build up. In a greenhouse, keep the concrete free of algae by regular scrubbing or the use of cleaning fluids. In a conservatory the flooring should be non-slip. Choose flooring materials such as decorative non-slip ceramic tiles, a vinyl floor covering, sealed cork tiles, or woven seagrass or coconut matting with a latex backing.

Untidiness inside the greenhouse or conservatory can be a danger when children are scrambling about and playing. There are numerous options for shelving, and for tiered or bench staging for displays of plants and pots. Always store chemicals, plant foods, composts and tools well out of the reach of small hands, and keep the floors, paths and doorways clear and free of potential hazards.

SECURE BOUNDARIES

Secure boundaries keep unwanted visitors out, stop nosey neighbours peering in and, most importantly, ensure that inquisitive young children are prevented from wandering into the road. They also provide shelter from winds and can form an attractive backdrop for the rest of the garden: just think how much improved a picture looks once it has been framed. A secure boundary needs careful thought. The ideal answer is solid fencing, with a child-proof gate. However, as your time and budget may not stretch to this, the solution may be to repair or replace parts of existing fencing as necessary.

The first step, then, is a close inspection – is the boundary working? If not, what is the problem? There may be some gaping holes at the bottom of a hedge, a broken fence panel, or walls that need re-pointing. At worst, it may be painfully obvious that the whole boundary needs replacing. Before you start work, you must establish to whom it belongs. As a general rule, the person on whose side the fence posts are, owns the boundary, and there is joint responsibility for the one at the bottom of the garden. This guide does not help with clarifying the ownership of hedges, however, and you may

Left: Effective garden boundaries provide privacy and security.

ABOVE: Bricks are the best form of boundary but they are expensive so make the most of a brick wall by decorating it.

have to consult the deeds of the house – and those of your neighbours – to establish this.

Renovating or replacing boundaries should be the first job that you tackle before starting on the rest of the garden. It is hard but important work, and, if well-planned, should cause the minimum of disturbance to flower beds and shrubs.

WALLS

A wall makes the most impressive boundary. If you are lucky enough to have one, it is well worth looking after. If a wall is unstable, leaning or bowed out in places, then you will probably need to enlist the help of a professional in order to repair it. If the mortar between the bricks – and perhaps the odd brick itself – has crumbled, you can replace the bricks and have the wall re-pointed.

Climbing plants such as ivy will do no harm to a wall that is sound, and can be an extremely attractive addition to the boundary, but if the wall is weak the plant's strong roots will exploit the cracks.

Painting a wall in a bold colour such as blue or yellow can look striking in a small backyard, and covers up a multitude of sins. A single-coloured background will give scope for all sorts of dramatic colour combinations, or if you feel creative you could have fun with a mural. Weather-proof masonry paint should be used outside: this is very tough and will last well, reducing the need for re-painting.

BELOW: Lightweight fences and sturdy trellises create screens that can be used effectively to create dens or, alternatively, to protect your delicate plantings in other parts of the garden.

TYPES OF FENCING

ABOVE: An interwoven fence.

ABOVE: Trellis.

ABOVE: Close-boarded fence.

ABOVE: Chain-link fence.

ABOVE: Lapped fence.

ABOVE: Picket fence.

FENCES

Fences make instant boundaries and take up very little growing space. They are expensive when compared with the cost of a hedge, however, and also deteriorate over the years whereas a hedge improves with age.

One of the most common problem with old fences is that they start to sag and lean. Leaning fences are usually a result of one or two posts rotting in the soil. The easiest way to fix them so that they stand upright again is with concrete spurs, which are bolted to the sound, upper part of the post. Start by supporting the fence panels on either side with bricks, then saw off the post just above ground level. Dig out the remains of the old stump, and then re-fill the hole with soil and hardcore, ramming this in as tightly as possible. Bolt the spur to the post using galvanised coach bolts. If you have to replace the whole post, dig out the old stump and ram in a short metal spike, designed to support fence posts, and install

the new fence post. Individual fence panels can also be replaced, and the new colour disguised by painting it with an appropriately coloured wood stain and planting a climber against it. Some traditional wood preservatives such as creosote are poisonous to plants, but there are newer ones on the market that will not harm plants. To ensure a level finish, make sure that you ram in the soil as firmly as possible, and check the vertical and horizontal planes of the panel with a spirit level.

Wire-mesh or chain-link fencing

This type of fencing could be a cost-effective solution for keeping a toddler within bounds. The fence need only be 1–1.5m (3½–5ft) high, and could be covered with quick-growing summer climbers such as sweet peas, then slower growing evergreens for the winter. This fencing would make a child-safe area.

RIGHT: An effective combination of simple timber poles and vigorous shrub roses makes this boundary difficult to penetrate after about three years' growth. In early summer and autumn the flowers, followed by the hips, provide a splash of colour. The scheme has the added advantages of being simple to maintain and inexpensive to create.

Hurdles

Hurdles are traditionally woven willow fences that were used as sheep pens. They can be used in gardens as a temporary fence either while waiting for a hedge to mature, or in their own right. They make a natural-looking backdrop for plants.

An additional benefit for environmentally conscious consumers is that the use of willow for hurdles – unlike many other wooden products – does not require the destruction of natural woodlands because it is harvested annually as a renewable crop in a traditional form of coppicing. The wetlands in which willow trees grow are internationally important as environmentally sensitive areas. The trees grow there naturally, and the aquatic wildlife is protected and left undisturbed apart from the annual harvest.

Hurdles are ideal for fencing, forming natural protection by filtering the wind and sheltering plants. They will last for several years, gradually turning a silver-grey in colour.

HEDGES

For a garden in a windy spot, a hedge may well be the best solution for providing a degree of shelter. Fences and walls are of no use as windbreaks, because when wind meets a solid barrier it tends to go up and over it and down the other side, often increasing in speed. Hedges make much more efficient windbreaks because they filter the wind, reducing its impact rather than trying to stop it altogether. However, even the fastest-growing hedges take time to make a decent boundary. A classy compromise is to erect a woven-willow hurdle fence behind a newly planted hedge.

Saving hedges

Whether an existing hedge is worth saving depends on what it is, how much you like it and what state it is in. Cut back plants such as box, holly, laurel and privet by half to rejuvenate the hedge. Conifers will not re-grow from old wood but yew responds well, growing back more bushy. If there are gaps or bare stems at the bottom of a hedge, plant something else in front. The filler plants must be tough, and tolerant of dry, often shady soil. Plants such as the Oregon grape (*Mahonia aquifolium*) and a spurge (*Euphorbia wulfenii*) would be ideal: these are fast-growing, tough and evergreen. Ensure that they receive extra rations of water during the

ABOVE: Using hedges as internal garden boundaries makes a garden more exciting for children to explore.

first season after planting so that they get well-established; a hedge is a greedy and thirsty neighbour with which to contend. If you are in a hurry to plug gaps, you can use plastic-mesh netting as a temporary measure.

If you resort to a short-back-and-sides to rejuvenate a hedge, and you have young children to keep in, then you will need to add an alternative secure structure. This is another wonderful opportunity for using woven-willow hurdles, but trellising or chain-link fencing might be a cheaper option.

Types of hedges

FORMAL: This is usually made up of a single type of plant, although a mixture could be used (and look very attractive) if different species that grow at the same rate were selected.

It is clipped regularly, and has a neat, uniform appearance. Examples include beech, box, lawson cypress (*Chamaecyparis lawsoniana*), leyland cypress (x *Cupressocyparis leylandii*), privet and western red cedar (*Thuja plicata*).

INFORMAL: The bushes or shrubs in this hedge are left to grow naturally, or are cut back only occasionally. This means a lot less work than for a formal hedge, and often the benefit of magnificent flowering displays. The major drawback is that it takes up a lot of space and is only suitable for large gardens. An informal hedge may consist of a single species or a mixture of plants. Good evergreen examples include barberry *(Berberis x stenophylla)*, a plant with arching prickly stems and fabulous golden-yellow flowers in mid-spring; laurustinus *(Viburnum tinus)*, a common favourite that seems to thrive anywhere and flowers in the winter when anything is a bonus; and an upright cotoneaster (*C. simonsii*) which has small white flowers in spring, and bright red berries in autumn. As

SUITABLE HEDGES FOR CHILDREN AND ANIMALS	
Box (*Buxus sempervirens*): a small, dense hedge	
with evergreen leaves. Use the dwarf	30cm (1ft)
B.s. Suffruiticosa for low hedging.	15cm (6in)
Western red cedar (*Thuja plicata*):	
'Atrovirens' has bright green foliage.	75cm (30in)
The Lawson cypress (*Chamaecyparis lawsoniana*): particularly 'Green Hedger' which has rich green colour.	75cm (30in)
Beech (*Fagus sylvatica*): hangs on to its russet brown dead leaves all winter. Needs light well-drained soil.	45cm (18in)
Hornbeam (*Carpinus betulis*): similar to beech but better suited to heavy clay soil.	45cm (18in)

ABOVE: Lilac makes a very impressive flowering hedge and is wonderfully scented.

an extra deterrent to escaping children you may prefer a thorny subject: pyracantha fits the bill nicely, being thorny and evergreen, with a magnificent berry display in autumn, or, if you do not mind bare stems in winter, a magnificent rose called 'Queen Elizabeth' will form a hedge approximately 1.5m (5ft) high.

How to buy plants

Hedging plants may be bought in pots or with just a ball of soil wrapped in sacking, or as specimens with bare roots. The latter is by far the cheapest option, and size-for-size will establish just as fast. Bare-root bushes must be planted in the dormant season, but this is no great drawback as it is the best time of year for planting. Conifers tend to be sold root-balled, while beech, privet and hawthorn tend to be sold with bare roots.

Trimming hedges

Conifer hedges should only be trimmed when they reach the required height, then the sides and top should be pruned annually in late summer. If you use a powered hedge trimmer, make sure that you wear protective clothing and there are no children running around. This is also a good time to prune other slow-growing evergreens in the garden. Faster-growing hedge species should be pruned regularly in summer.

CHAPTER TWO

A GARDEN TO PLAY IN

No matter what you do, children will stamp their mark all over the garden, investigating every corner. For a happy life, the garden should not only be made as safe as possible for them – by implementing a range of measures already discussed – but should also be planned to maximise the space in which children can play. They will make the most of whatever size garden is on offer and, although there is more scope for adventure and for certain types of games – such as hide-and-seek – in a large garden that has plenty of secret nooks and crannies, it is surprising how absorbed a child can become in the make-believe world of something small, such as a miniature garden planted in a tyre and kept on a balcony.

ABOVE: Trees not only provide privacy from neighbours, they are also great fun for children to play in.

OPPOSITE: Natural curiosity means that children will investigate every garden feature. Remember that games of make-believe keep children entertained for hours on end.

PLAY AREAS

Games involving equipment are not necessarily the most enjoyable or interesting for children. Imaginary games are very important, and very popular. Make-believe situations such as being stranded on an island and having to make a home and find food (even if it does involve raiding the

BELOW: Picket fencing is an excellent form of fencing for creating an internal garden boundary. It has been used here to fence in the adult area of the garden, leaving the children with a wide open area to play in.

kitchen) will keep children occupied for hours. The only equipment needed for a game like this will be a few recyclable items such as an old sheet, a large box and a few bits and pieces from the kitchen.

Running and chasing games are as much fun as imaginary ones, and this is where a lawn is invaluable. The ideal family garden to suit young children will have as much uncluttered lawn space as possible. Flower beds are really something of a luxury at this stage; when the children are older you can re-design and increase these and the borders.

A patio or firm surface is as important as the lawn, if not more so. Whereas after a day of heavy rain the lawn will remain wet and soggy, a paved area will start to dry out straight away, making it a useful place for games. It is also a good surface to play on with anything that has wheels, starting with baby walkers and graduating up to toy tractors and tricycles. A paved area is also ideal for marbles, and for the smooth operation of toy push chairs and cars, hopefully freeing up space in the living room and kitchen. Paved areas are invaluable.

If you have space in the garden to set aside a specific play area it is sure to become an important ally, particularly when children are small. You can put them in it and let them play, knowing that they are safe, secure and occupied. For the play-area boundary, use low fencing such as chain-link or, for a more decorative feature, a little picket fence.

Children adore digging and would love to be allowed to dig holes all over the lawn. To satisfy this craving, give them a patch of their own – perhaps a sandpit, a part of a flower bed or a large tub garden. Digging in soil is particularly satisfying: there are mud pies to be made and the added excitement of discovering soil life such as worms and beetles.

Children are instantly attracted to water, and during a long hot summer it is really almost a necessity. Children love getting wet and splashing around. If the use of a hose is

permitted, a sprinkler inspires squeals of delight. Otherwise, the safest option is probably a simple plastic paddling pool that can be supervised, then put away after use.

POSITIONING PLAY AREAS

Play areas for small children should be in sight of the window of the most-used room of the house, and close enough for you to hear the cries if a tumble or accident occurs. Never put a swing, slide or climbing frame on concrete. Provide a base of grass, bark chippings or play matting.

As children grow older they will appreciate somewhere that provides them with a little privacy, and this is when tree-houses, Wendy houses and dens become popular. The clever use of plants can provide secret areas. Stepping stones leading to a small clearing made in a shrub border, with a floor of bark mulch and a couple of logs for seats, would make a magical meeting place.

ABOVE: This quality playhouse would provide at least five or six years of play for most children, and with a garden patch to cultivate in front, it is a child's dream home come true. Later, the playhouse could be used as a potting shed or for storing furniture.

RIGHT: Smooth concrete pavers and a packet of coloured chalk encourage artistic expression. The pictures will fade away naturally or can be washed off with a garden hose.

PLAY EQUIPMENT

If you have ever wished for children's play equipment that does not cost a huge amount of money, is not painted in garish colours, and does not look as though it has been borrowed from the local playing field, you could always build it yourself. If you do decide to go along the DIY route, it is particularly worthwhile making good, solid, sturdy structures that will have a long and useful life, and which could be adapted for use after children have finished with them. You might, for instance, want to have a go at making a swing, a sandpit or climbing frame that is a decorative feature in its own right.

It is, of course, important that home-made equipment is strong, sturdy and steady, that all wood is sanded down and coated with exterior-grade varnish, and that nails and screws are safely sunk below the surface. Any ready-made play equipment that you buy should have been made to approved standards, and you should check over and maintain everything on a regular basis.

Most families inevitably end up acquiring one or more manufactured pieces of play equipment for children. The plastic components and dazzling colours of many such items will probably seem at first to be a garish intrusion in your garden, but hopefully the pleasure that the equipment gives will outweigh the eyesore factor. Live with it for two or three years until the children have outgrown it, and then sell it or give it away. On the plus side, plastic does have certain advantages: it is tough, light, weather-proof and safe, and has no sharp or rough edges. Plastic play equipment is also generally less expensive than comparable ready-made wooden structures for children.

ABOVE AND LEFT: Standard play houses customised by adding shutters and painting with an oil-based paint.

OPPOSITE: Although large, this fantastic design is in keeping with the house.

SWINGS

Play equipment that will be used for several years, such as a swing, should be carefully sited, and can then be softened or disguised to become a garden feature. For example, after many years of heavy use, a swing made from sturdy timber could be enhanced and incorporated into the flower garden by having some attractive climbers grown up it. A vigorous clematis such as the yellow-flowered species *Clematis tangutica,* or *C. montana,* one of the easiest and toughest, would soon scramble its way over the frame. Both of these plants are deciduous, but there is also an evergreen species, *C. armandii,* which has glossy green leaves and spectacular white flowers in mid-spring. Swings made from tubular steel are cost-effective, but should have the supports concreted into the ground to make the structure stable.

ABOVE: This type of assault course is constructed from two sturdy posts, a length of quality rope and a harness attached to a strong metal ring clip that slides along freely. Do not attempt this on the washing line!

SANDPITS

A sandpit is great fun for toddlers, and provides lots of digging in what should be reasonably hygienic conditions.

There are many types available, the most common being the bright-blue plastic variety that comes with a fitted lid. All sandpits must have a cover of some sort, to stop the sand

LEFT AND RIGHT: This is a strong, rustic arch constructed from two sturdy uprights and a cross-bar. It can support a rope or swing, or even both, and provide a substantial structure for climbing plants, eventually becoming a full-time arbour or flowering archway.

BELOW AND RIGHT: A sandpit is one of the easiest pieces of play equipment to construct and then adapt later on. A lid is important to protect the sand from the weather and local cats. The timber decking lid makes an attractive feature in its own right.

from becoming too wet in the rain and to prevent any visiting cats from using it as a dirt tray.

For a temporary sandpit, an old lorry or tractor tyre is difficult to beat for simplicity. Tyre centres are usually more than happy to give away old tyres for free. Give the tyre a good scrub with some hot, soapy water to get rid of the oil and dirt, then apply a coat of paint in a nice bright colour. Place it on a sheet of plastic, punctured with holes to allow drainage, then fill it up with sand. This should be silver sand, not builder's sand: although it is rather expensive and the tyre will take more than you think, silver sand is worth using because it does not stain clothes and drains easily. Add a bucket and spade, and away the children can go. The tyre sandpit will be the perfect size for providing hours of enter-

tainment for small hands, and there is a ready-made seat all the way around, too, that is useful for turning out sandcastles and is also easy to sweep the sand from.

PLAY HOUSES

The cheapest play houses are made from cloth or PVC . They have tough, tubular support frames and come in a range of bright colours. More expensive, but much more durable and equally colourful, are play houses made from rigid plastic. Using a tent as a temporary camp can satisfy almost the same needs as a play house. The advantages are that a tent is generally cheaper than a wooden play house, and if well looked after, will survive longer than the cheaper cloth or plastic play houses.

LAWNS

The family lawn causes more work and more worry than any other part of the garden. We walk, run and play on it in all kinds of weather, tearing the turf, compacting the soil and generally giving it a hard life. With a little know-how you can keep the lawn green and growing by mowing and feeding, and by carrying out the occasional repair job. Whereas most plants grow from their tips, grass grows from the base, and this is how it copes with being continually cut, providing an endless supply of fresh green shoots. To keep a lawn in good condition, the most important factor by far is a regular mowing regime. How often it needs cutting will depend on the weather and on the type of lawn you wish to have: the ideal height of cut for a family lawn is 4–5cm (1½–2in); a lawn of this type will need mowing about once every 10 days in the height of the growing season. A fine bowling green, on the other hand, would need mowing almost every day.

You should cut any long-grass areas – left to create mini-meadows – in midsummer, after the wild flowers have set seed. To use an area like this as a rough lawn for the rest of the summer, follow this with two more cuts one month apart. Bear in mind that an ordinary lawnmower will not be able to cope with this sort of maintenance. If you have only small areas of long grass you will be able to cut them with a strimmer, but for a larger meadow you will need a rotary mower. This is expensive to buy and can be costly to service and repair, but will pay its way in the long term. Alternatively, you should be able to rent a rotary mower at a reasonable daily rate from a local hire shop.

Lawns are not good for people with allergies because the pollen grains from grasses and dust from mowings aggravate the allergy. If a lawn is unavoidable, the allergic person should stay inside during the day when mowing takes place and a cylinder mower that collects clippings should be used.

Left: The lawn copes with a punishing schedule imposed by a young, active family. The two most important ways to keep it growing vigorously are to mow it regularly and to avoid physical games in wet weather.

ABOVE: Lawns are invaluable spaces for ball games. Keep your lawn as uncluttered as possible to ensure maximum space and minimum damage.

SHADY LAWNS

Lawns grow reasonably well in semi-shade but they find it very tough growing under trees, where a combination of shade, dry soil and poor nutrition means only moss seems able to grow. Tackle the problem by removing a few of the lower branches, keeping the area well watered and cutting the grass less frequently so it is left to grow slightly longer. Re-seed in the autumn after spiking all over, and use a proprietary seed mixture designed for shady sites. It will contain a percentage of woodland grasses. It is pointless to try and establish grass under large forest trees, such as oak, ash or beech; it is better to grow shade-loving ground-cover plants.

MAKING A NEW LAWN

A new lawn can be created from either turf or seed. For a family lawn that needs to be put to use as soon as possible, laying turf is the best option because it establishes much more quickly than a lawn grown from seed. Whichever method you use, the ground preparations are very similar.

It is crucial at this stage to eliminate perennial weeds such as dandelions, docks, couch grass and bindweed, which have long, tough roots. The organic way to get rid of them is to dig them out, or to cover the area with thick carpet or plastic sheeting, leaving it in place for a growing season to smother them. Shortlived annual weeds can be simply hoed off.

SEED

Growing a lawn from seed has the advantage of allowing a particular choice of grass mixtures to be selected. It is also cheaper than turf. A major disadvantage, however, is that seed germination can be slow and erratic, making it more difficult to establish a lawn successfully. This is a serious drawback for the family garden which has to cope with instant wear and tear, as the lawn will remain delicate for between nine and 12 months. The real value of seed in the family garden is for patching up problem areas.

Seed mixtures

A general-purpose lawn is required for a family garden, and if children are to use it as a play area, a hardwearing mixture is essential. There is a bewildering variety of grass-seed mixtures on the market for every conceivable situation, which – instead of making things easier – can end up being more confusing. The first question is whether or not to select a

---

PREPARING THE GROUND

1 First of all, dig or fork over the soil thoroughly: this will break it up, and create a better structure by allowing air in and water to drain away. Next, level the area roughly using a rake.

2 Walk all over the soil on your heels (this technique is commonly known as the "gardener's shuffle") to firm the soil, to settle any uneven levels, and to fill hollows and flatten bumps.

3 Rake in a suitable fertilizer, applying a generous handful per square metre (sq yd), then rake again to create a final, firm level. Leave to settle for one week before sowing or laying turf.

SOWING FROM SEED

1 Use string to divide the area into 1m (1yd) strips, and divide these into 1m (1yd) lengths. Move the canes along the strips as you sow.

2 Use a small container that holds enough seed for 1sq m (1 sq yd). Scatter the seeds evenly.

3 Hire a seed distributor if you need to sow a large area. Lightly rake the seed into the surface. Water regularly.

SEED MIXTURES

A seed mixture for a family lawn should contain the following grasses in approximate proportions.

3 PARTS DWARF PERENNIAL RYE GRASS (*Lolium perenne*)
Hardwearing and quick to establish.

4 PARTS FINE FESCUE (*Festuca*)
These grasses that make up a luxury lawn are quick to establish, but are rather delicate and easily pushed out by stronger grasses.

1 PART BROWNTOP BENT (*Agrostis canina*)
A fine-leaved grass that is slow to establish but eventually forms a neat, dense turf.

2 PARTS SMOOTH-STALKED MEADOW GRASS (*Poa*)
A creeping grass that, once established, is hardwearing and resistant to dry weather.

Asthmatics: All lawns must be cut regularly to look good and stay healthy. If there is an asthmatic in the family a grass lawn should pose no problem because the grasses do not get a chance to flower. Areas of long grass, such as in a wildlife garden, should be avoided.

mixture with rye grass (*Lolium perenne*), which is extremely tough and resilient, and is quick to germinate. A major drawback, however, is that it needs cutting more often than other grasses. Luckily, new dwarf varieties of rye grass are a useful addition to the durability required of a family lawn.

TURF

Turf will cost more than seed initially, but it does give an instant visual effect and can be used much sooner, although it still needs time for the turves to knit themselves together. Timing is important because turf will not store for more than a few days. If you were to order some for the weekend and it rained continuously, then the job would still have to be done. The best time of the year is the autumn, when the soil is still warm and there is likely to be plenty of rain. You can lay turf in the spring, once the weather has warmed up, but watch out for dry spells. Ask to see a sample before you buy a large amount of turf. Check for uniform thickness and for good overall colour.

LAYING TURF

1 Lay the first row of turves along the edge of the area, and press them closely together. Check that they are even by using a spirit level on a board laid across the new turf.

2 Working from a board placed on the first row, lay the turves in straight lines, staggering the pieces along the rows and ending with a half- or full-sized piece on the edge.

3 To even out any bumps or hollows, lift the turf and then add or remove as much soil as is necessary. When you are satisfied with the level, gently tap the turves in place.

4 Make up a 50:50 mixture of good garden soil or loam compost mixed with sand. Spread this along the cracks, and gently work it in by sweeping over the grass with a broom or the back of a rake.

5 Carefully trim the edges of the turf, using a half-moon edging iron or a sharp spade.

ABOVE: A lawn can create a sense of space and provides a wonderful area for children to play.

RENOVATING A NEGLECTED LAWN

A lawn that is left to its own devices will quickly become overgrown. Lawns that have been neglected in this way are a common problem for new owners of a property.

MOWING

The first job is to cut the grass and then to keep it cut. Long grass cannot be cut by the average lawnmower, so you may need to hire a machine from a local shop. If the grass is longer than knee height, you will need a petrol-driven brush-cutter or strimmer to reduce it to a manageable length. You will then be able to cut it down further using a rotary mower that is designed to cut grass up to about 30cm (12in).

When using these powerful machines, wear protective clothing. You cannot see what obstructions are lying hidden in the long grass, and the blades of a mower can hurl out objects at terrific speed. Cut the grass in dry weather; if there is too much moisture, grass clogs the blades.

Do not be tempted to cut the grass down to the finished height all in one go. Cut it down to about 15cm (6in) first, then leave it to recover and green up again for a couple of weeks before you use your own mower on it. Set the mower at the highest cut, and reduce it by only about 1.5cm (a good ½in) for each subsequent mowing. Leave the grass to green up between each mowing, but aim to finish by cutting once a week during the height of the growing season. At first the lawn may be full of coarse grasses, but regular mowing should kill them, allowing the lawn grasses to take over.

BARE PATCHES

Bare patches in a lawn may be caused by a number of factors, such as the removal of weeds or dog's urine, but the most common problem is too much wear and tear throughout the year. If damage keeps occurring in the same place, consider alternatives to grass, such as ground-cover plants for shady areas, and perhaps stepping stones for an informal path.

ABOVE: *Stepping stones can be usefully employed to cover up problem bare patches. Ensure the stones are sunk below grass level so the mower blades can pass safely over.*

Fixing bare patches

Small patches are simple to re-seed, whereas larger patches can be either seeded or turfed. First square off the bare patch, removing any loose pieces of turf, and then break up the soil surface using a fork. Using your heels, firm the soil lightly all over, and rake it level.

CARING FOR YOUR LAWN

ABOVE: Lawns benefit from a regular raking to remove dead grass.

ABOVE: Aerating with a fork loosens the soil and gets air into the roots.

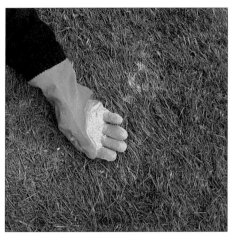

ABOVE: If your lawn is in poor condition, apply lawn feed.

Either lay turf in place, fitting it together like a jigsaw, or sow grass seed at 25–35g (1–1½oz) per 1 square metre (sq yd). This is roughly equivalent to two handfuls of seed, and if you put your feet as wide apart as you can and lean forwards as far as possible, you will cover about 1 square metre (sq yd). Grass seed should be sown in early spring or autumn, when wet weather can be expected and the soil is warm.

RAKING

Every so often, the lawn will benefit from a vigorous raking to remove the dead layer of grass that accumulates among the roots. This scarifying allows better drainage and air circulation. It should be done in early autumn, to give the grass time to recover before the winter. Use a lawn or garden rake, or hire a powered scarifier from a local hire shop.

AERATING

Grass roots need air to breathe in order to stay healthy, and air spaces that allow water to drain through. However, air is easily squashed out of the soil.

The simplest way to aerate a small lawn is to drive a garden fork at least 7.5cm (3in) into it, and to rock it back and forth gently before pulling it out vertically. Leave about 15cm (6in) between the lines of holes. This is hard work, so take your time. Motorised spikers make the job easy, and they are well worth hiring for a large lawn. For large areas on heavy soils, a hollow tine fork, which takes out a core of earth and leaves an air channel, can be used, although this tool should only be used once every few years. Early autumn is the best time to spike, allowing the lawn to benefit over the wet winter months, but the job can be carried out in spring.

TOP DRESSING

To encourage dense growth and level out small bumps and hollows, a top dressing is the answer. After raking or spiking, apply a mixture of loam with a generous helping of potting compost and sand (if your soil is on the heavy side, increase the amount of sand). Place small piles of the top dressing evenly over the surface, then use the back of a rake to work it into the soil, finishing off with a light brushing.

USING TREES

Trees are wonderful things. They muffle the harsh sounds of city life, clean the air and give us oxygen to breathe. They provide homes and shelter to insects and animals, and they shade us from the sun. If you have a large, mature tree in your garden, you should consider yourself very lucky.

In a small garden, however, you might not see a big, old tree as quite such a blessing, with its hungry roots sucking all the moisture from the soil and the canopy shading out what little sun you get. But if you accept it and work with the subject, you can turn the disadvantages into something positive. Children can have hours of fun playing on swings, ropes and hammocks suspended from the branches. You can hang bird-feeders and install bird and bat boxes, and even develop a new hobby studying the wildlife that uses the tree.

Trees do have an immense thirst, so anything that will be in competition with the root area must be chosen carefully. A lawn is out of the question, and plants should be adaptable to dry, shady conditions. Trees also drop vast quantities of leaves. Collect them to make nutritious leaf mould: pile them into a compost bin or in a spare corner of the garden, or fill plastic dustbin liners and store them out of the way. It takes at least a year for leaves to rot down into usable leaf mould, but it is well worth the wait.

PLANTS FOR DRY SHADE UNDER TREES
The Oregon grape (*Mahonia aquifolium*) is a shrub that does well in dry shade. It has an upright, structural shape with evergreen leaves, and lovely yellow (usually scented) flowers

RIGHT: *This mature tree seems to be tailor-made for a child's swing. It is certainly strong and supple enough. The branches should be given a thorough once over, checking that the bark is healthy and there is no sign of diseased or weakened areas. Protect the bark from becoming damaged by cushioning the rope with a piece of old carpet.*

ABOVE: A tree-platform is good fun for older children. Here, sturdy pieces of wood off-cuts are nailed across the centre bough. The rope ladder can be rolled up once the children are in. The pirates' flag completes the scene.

at the end of the winter, just when we need cheering up. Portugal laurel (*Prunus lusitanica*) – a large shrub useful for screening – has lovely glossy, oval, evergreen leaves with red leaf stalks.

Many bulbs are perfect for planting under deciduous trees because they do most of their growing early in the year before the tree is in full leaf. Cyclamen, daffodils, lily-of-the-valley, snowdrops and windflowers will all thrive. For herbaceous flowering plants, try columbine (*Aquilegia*), Siberian bugloss (*Brunnera macrophylla*) and fringecup (*Tellima grandiflora*).

If all else fails, plant one of the ivy varieties or periwinkle – both are evergreen – to make a neat, flat carpet. Periwinkles give a good display of blue flowers in late spring. The species *Vinca major* grows about 30cm (12in) tall and spreads very quickly, although it is easily cut back to keep under control. *Vinca minor* is less of a bully, and is shorter, growing almost flat on the soil surface.

USING TREES FOR PLAY

It is surprising how strong and supple the branches are if a tree is healthy; only dead or weakened branches are likely to snap under pressure. For a branch to be strong enough to support a small child on a swing, it should have a minimum diameter of approximately 15cm (6in); this will usually only be found on trees that are at least 50 years old.

Before allowing children to play on any tree, give it a close inspection to make sure that it is safe. Look for signs of damage or disease, such as the appearance of fungi or gummy resins on the trunk, which might indicate problems. Position ropes, swings and ladders on large, healthy branches, as near to the trunk as is feasible (where branches are stronger) but not so close that a child might accidentally crash into it. To prevent ropes from chafing and damaging the branch, place a piece of rubber matting or carpet between the rope and branch. Check both the rope and the branch regularly for signs of wear and tear. If you have a tree that is not quite large enough to support the full weight of play equipment, a climbing frame that is securely attached to a tree would be ideal; children could then scramble from one to the other.

A tree-house is the ultimate piece of play equipment, providing a private fantasy world. It is important to have a strong platform made of planks or exterior-grade plywood, which should be nailed to the centre of a branch after being checked for splinters, old nails and staples. Distribute the load across as many branches as possible, and surround the

ABOVE: A hammock will give hours of fun, but make sure that it is hung from two strong supports.

platform with a barrier. A temporary house can be made from an old sheet or a tent, suspended from the branches above. If you get carried away with more permanent roofing and additional features, the tree-house will be even more popular, and also comfortable for a night spent outside.

The best surface under trees used for playing is wood chip, which looks natural and is hardwearing yet soft to land on. There are different grades available, varying from fine to coarse. The coarse type lasts longest and is ideal for play surfaces. There are also different colours of wood chip: some

of the brighter ones may take some getting used to, but they can look very effective in the right situation.

Hammocks are a taste of luxury popular with all ages, providing a relaxing place to absorb the garden atmosphere once you have fought off any rivals. If only one branch is in a convenient position, erect a fence post for the other end, or buy a hammock with its own frame.

Children love weeping trees that they can crawl under and hide in. A Kilmarnock willow (*Salix caprea* 'Kilmarnock') provides an instant weeping effect. It grows no taller than 2m (6½ft), and the curtain of branches grows thicker every year. Thin these from beneath every few years, to prevent them from growing top-heavy.

WILDLIFE CORNER

A garden should be a place of fantasy as well as a place for learning and, if you garden with wildlife in mind, you will create an ideal setting for both. A wildlife garden will have hidden and unexpected nooks and crannies that are likely to be as appealing to children as they are to other creatures. The result of a little thought and careful selection of plants will be a huge, living museum right on your doorstep, from which children will derive immeasurable benefit. Children have a natural curiosity for everything around them, and are fascinated by the living world. It is important that they start to understand the basics of nature while they are young, to realise how food chains work, how plants and trees grow, and where creatures live.

Make your policy "live and let live", and think long and hard before killing anything or tidying up vegetation. Make it a point of interest to check on how the local greenfly population is faring instead of reaching for a spray; it will be fascinating to watch the ladybirds move in, and to see how the natural order of events unfolds.

The ideal design for a wildlife garden is a woodland glade with long grass at the edge containing wild flowers, leading to shrubs and trees. A majestic oak tree would be too large for most back gardens, but there are several small native trees from which to choose. A silver birch is probably the best all-rounder. It is relatively small but extremely graceful and, although deciduous, has beautiful bark to look at during the winter months.

Fruit trees – such as apples, pears and mulberries – are also a good choice. They will produce lovely blossom in the spring, followed by fruit that can be shared: pick the best and leave the rest for smaller creatures to enjoy.

LEFT: *This birdbath mosaic nestles in a bed of marigolds and wallflowers, making a colourful and surprising point of interest in the garden for both birds and children.*

RIGHT: *The entry hole of a birdhouse should be positioned where it is sheltered from the weather.*

ABOVE: Leaving a patch of grass to develop as a mini-meadow creates a different environment for children to experience, and it attracts insects, butterflies and birds.

It is best to choose as many native plants as possible, particularly trees and shrubs, as they provide food and shelter for a wide variety of insects and birds. For an evergreen, it is difficult to beat the merits of holly, which provides a home and food for hundreds of different insects and birds. Holly has separate male and female plants, so you will need both to get berries. One male for several females will do. Common ivy is a very underrated plant. Not only is it evergreen, but

it thrives in just about any aspect and situation, and will grow up almost any vertical surface without the need for wires or string. It provides cover for birds and shelter for insects. The end-of-year flowers are rich in nectar for late-flying insects, and the berries provide a feast for birds when other wild foods are becoming scarce.

The addition of water to a garden will more than double the number of species that visit. Water can be a danger when children are small, but a birdbath kept topped up, or a small pebble fountain, can provide a welcome watering spot for all sorts of creatures to bathe and drink from.

Birds are a pleasure to invite into the garden. Put up a bird-feeding station – even just one peanut feeder hanging from a tree – and they will come flocking in. Hang feeders in a position that is visible from a window in the house, away from overhanging branches from which stalking cats could pounce, and the birds will provide hours of entertainment.

Inviting birds to feed is easy, but attracting them to nest is another matter. To be appealing to birds, a nesting box must be located in a territory that is well supplied with food for rearing offspring. To make up for a lack of large, old trees, position bird boxes on walls or fences in a shady spot that is reasonably well-hidden but still allows easy access.

Allow an area of long grass to develop, carrying out the first cut of the year in late summer, then cutting regularly until the end of the year. You will be surprised by the number of wild flowers that appear as if by magic, the seeds having lain dormant in the soil for years.

A pile of logs in a corner will provide shelter for animals such as hibernating frogs, toads, newts and, if you are lucky, hedgehogs, as well as being the ideal place for creatures called decomposers which feed on rotting wood, recycling it into the soil. A compost bin is another habitat for decomposers, and is an integral part of any environmental garden, recycling organic material ready for it to be returned to the soil.

SPACE FOR BALL GAMES

As well as being a feature of many children's games, playing with a ball is an important developmental skill in a child's co-ordination. For ball games, children need an uncluttered space.

Lawns or flat, grassy areas are suitable for many ball games, especially those in which children are likely to fling

BELOW: Ball games in an unsuitable garden can create havoc. Children need plenty of space, well away from delicate plants and structures.

themselves after a bouncing ball. For games where ball bounce is vital, hard surfaces are required. A ballpark area can be cleverly incorporated into the design of a garden by changing surface textures to indicate the boundary. For instance, cobblestones set low into concrete will subtly restrict the area of play, and could also be used below or near windows, gateways and other hazardous areas to prevent any damage.

In a medium-sized garden, a circular or central lawn area will provide space for many different ball games, such as softball, tennis, scoopball, swingball and badminton. More vigorous games such as football and cricket could cause problems, because a central lawn does not have a backing wall against which balls can rebound, making damage to surrounding flower beds and garden structures more likely. For maximum play efficiency, the ideal lawn for games should be sited against a garden or garage wall which can take the brunt of hit and kicked balls, and on which goal posts can be marked. House walls are less suitable because the sound of the balls and the marks that they leave would be unacceptable. Windowless garage walls are ideal for basketball, which requires a hoop with a back board, and also for solo tennis practice or games of catch.

Trellis panels – set along the tops of low walls or free-standing – can be used to shield particularly delicate or exposed areas, or to prevent balls escaping from the garden. To stop balls from rolling on to flower beds, use raised bed edging or a low fence, but bear in mind that it will then be impossible to mow right up to the lawn edge, so a pair of hand shears or a strimmer will have to be used.

PLANTS FOR PLAY AREAS

Plants sited near ballpark areas should be chosen for their durability in withstanding flying balls and damage from children searching for lost balls. Plants with a tight or closed

ABOVE: The flower beds in this garden have been kept to a minimum at this stage, but when children get older the beds can develop into a more intricate design.

form, such as conifers, could be damaged permanently. Softer plants such as bamboos and other decorative grasses can be searched through easily, and ground-cover plants such as heathers, periwinkle and ivies can be trampled on. As woody stems and branches can be snapped and broken, choose plants that can produce growth and flowers each year from buds along the current year's stems – such as forsythia – not plants that are limited to flowering from a bud at the top of the stem, such as hydrangea.

Avoid plants with spines or thorns which might not initially frighten off older children, resulting in plenty of nasty cuts and scratches as they search for a lost ball or toy. It is also wise to avoid plants with big or soft leaves or delicate stems or flowers, which can easily be damaged. Deciduous plants are usually better able to recover from damage, as any scarred or torn leaves will be shed each year.

CYCLE TRACKS

Children often use a tricycle, bicycle or wheeled truck as soon as they are able to walk, then progress to bigger bikes, scooters and skates. To keep them happy, all-weather hard surfaces are an important feature of any family garden. For the safety of small children, this area should be sited close to the house so that they can be supervised. On a patio or terrace surface, children can safely master the skill of using anything on wheels, before venturing into the outside world.

Once your bikers are confident, they will want to be more adventurous. To encourage them to play in relative safety, a well-planned path or cycle track is the answer: this should be about 1m (3ft) wide to accommodate a bike moving at speed. For continuity, try to use the same surfacing material as that used for the patio or terrace.

A change of texture can be used to mark a particular track in a broader path. For example, a smooth track of pavers or engineering bricks can be laid firmly (in concrete) in the centre of a broader path made of more loosely laid brick pavers. Any cyclist will then be encouraged to keep to the track in the centre and away from any edging plants. Skaters and scooter-riders will require an especially broad and even surface of concrete or stable paving.

In a medium to large garden, a cycle track could be designed to encircle the garden, and weave among flower beds, shrubberies and the lawn, creating a route with exciting bends and hidden stretches. A sloping ramp would be fun for bikers as well as skaters. Before constructing a path, carefully consider its purpose, the wear and tear that it is likely to receive and the need for drainage. The secret of success is to build on a firm foundation. Whatever material you choose, you will need a slope or camber (raised centre) across the path to make sure that water runs off.

LEFT: A track around the garden edge saves wear and tear to the lawn and creates a safer environment for bikers than out on the road. Chopped bark blends well with the rest of the garden.

RIGHT: Toddlers on tricycles require a smooth surface and a ring of paving stones is ideal.

BARBECUES

Eating outside has become increasingly popular in the last few years, and barbecues are now a fixed part of the traditional summer scene.

The barbecue should be sited in a convenient place near the house so you do not have to traipse up and down clutching cooking utensils, crockery and food. Also consider any neighbours, and position the barbecue where smoke will not waft straight through their open windows. Finally, do not place it directly below overhanging trees or bushes which could catch light or suffer from intense heat.

ABOVE: *This is a permanent brick barbecue but you could easily make a similar one in loose bricks. An even simpler way to make a very basic barbecue at no cost at all is to make a pile of stones topped with chicken wire.*

ABOVE: *To make a loose barbecue, arrange the first layer of bricks on a hard, flat surface, leaving 5cm (2in) gaps between each one. Lay two more layers on top, staggering the joints. Place a sheet of mild steel, cut to size, over the bricks for burning the fuel, then continue stacking two more layers of bricks around the edge, leaving the front open. Fit a grill on which to cook – a reclaimed one from an old cooker is ideal. Add another two or three layers of bricks to form a windshield.*

There are many different types of barbecue available, from the basic firebox with a grill, to more expensive models which have added luxuries such as rotisseries, warming plates, cupboards and wheels.

If you do not relish the idea of learning bricklaying skills but intend to make good use of a barbecue, take the easy way out and make a semi-permanent one out of loose bricks. It is easy to make and even easier to dismantle. To make a full-size unit you will need about 100 bricks and a firebox/grill kit.

PETS IN THE GARDEN

If you garden in sympathy with wildlife, many uninvited yet welcome visitors will make use of your green oasis. You will also have a convenient place in which to keep domesticated animals that make excellent pets for children. The two most common garden pets are rabbits and guinea pigs, which soon become tame and are easily handled by children. They are both social animals, so it is unkind to keep them on their own. Two animals are only marginally more trouble than one, and if housed together they will keep each other company. Both species breed easily so, in order to avoid the likelihood of being overrun with the patter of tiny feet, keep two females together; two males sharing the same living space will probably fight.

THE HUTCH

The housing requirements for both rabbits and guinea pigs are virtually the same, although a guinea pig can live in a smaller hutch. Essentially, a hutch is a rectangular box with two or three compartments. It should be raised on legs at least 15cm (6in) tall, to allow for plenty of floor ventilation and to prevent easy access by predators. The roof should be protected from the extremes of weather with a bitumen or plastic covering, and should slightly overhang the sides. Inside, there should be a small sleeping compartment and a large living area, a corner of which will be taken over as a toilet. Use straw or woodshavings for covering the hutch floor. The front of the living area should be constructed of a mesh-covered frame that can be opened easily. The minimum dimensions for a single rabbit are about 1m (3ft) long, 45cm (18in) deep and 45cm (18in) high, but the larger you can make the hutch, the better it will be.

The best site for a hutch is in a sheltered position facing the morning sun, but do ensure that there is always some shade within the hutch so that the animals can retreat from direct sunshine without having to retire to their sleeping

ABOVE: Rabbits are social animals and require company and attention. They are ideal pets for children.

quarters. During very bad weather, a hutch will need a temporary plastic screen to shield it from driving winds and rain; in the wild, rabbits would normally be deep in their burrows during adverse weather conditions. Guinea pigs are less hardy than rabbits and need extra shelter during the winter. Move their hutch to a shed or outbuilding where extra heating can be supplied if necessary – this is particularly important at night when the temperature drops.

Space to run

Both rabbits and guinea pigs are grassland creatures, and so should have an enclosure of their own where they can enjoy fresh air, exercise and grazing. If the unit is portable it can be moved to different areas of the garden in rotation, providing fresh supplies of grass for your pets.

Rabbits and guinea pigs are vegetarians and will eat fruit and vegetable leftovers, as well as grass, hay and many flowering plants such as daisies and marigolds. Grass and hay are especially important to the diet of guinea pigs, and they should be given a constant supply. Supplement fresh food with rabbit pellets or guinea-pig grain from a pet shop, and provide constant access to fresh water from a bottle that releases a drink on demand.

Cleaning

Rabbits and guinea pigs are very clean animals, so if a hutch smells it is usually due to the owner's neglect. It will need regular cleaning to remove droppings and replace bedding.

CAT AND DOGS

Dogs can be trained to keep off flower beds, but they do need adequate lawn space to run and play on. Sensitive areas of the garden can be protected to a limited extent by strategic plantings of tough shrubs, or by fencing materials that blend well with the plants, such as green netting or chicken wire.

Cats soon make use of bare patches of soil for their toilet habits. Encourage them to use a specific area in the garden by making gravel or cat litter beds in appropriate spots.

RIGHT: Chickens, particularly bantams, also make good pets, with the added bonus of small eggs. The run is portable and can be moved around the garden to give the chickens plenty of fresh pickings.

SMALL GARDENS

In a small garden it is more important than ever to design carefully and make maximum use of the space available. Every little area in a small garden should be fully utilised. Plan for room to sit and eat outside, something to interest the children, and a careful selection of plants at all levels. To withstand the pressure of constant use, choose the best materials that you can afford for construction purposes. They should be robust and wear well, but still look good.

The surface material is the most crucial factor in the design of a small garden, and will directly influence how much use you will get from it. In a restricted area a lawn is out of the question, as it will probably receive only poor light and suffer from heavy use, which will cause nothing but problems. It is far better to concentrate on a surface that can be kept clean with the minimum of trouble, and used throughout the year in all types of weather.

SURFACES

Landscaping with hard materials is not something to take on lightly, as they are expensive and difficult to alter once in place. For this reason, think about the surface carefully before making a final choice. At least one advantage of a small patio area is that you may be able to afford to buy the best.

Test a sample before buying the full quantity, as materials can sometimes look totally different when they are laid down. Choose paving in colours and materials that are sympathetic

ABOVE: *Contrasting bricks can be used to create details such as this drum pattern which adds interest to a small patio.*

LEFT: *Even in a tiny garden you can incorporate features such as this sandpit.*

Above: A washing-up bowl is big enough for a mini-pond in which to keep tadpoles.

to your house; try to match brick colours and architectural details. Just as wooden decking would look out of place in front of a Victorian semi-detached house, so modern re-constituted paving would be wrong for a country cottage. Brick paving and real stone are two materials that do look good virtually anywhere. With little to rival them in both looks and versatility (they can be used in endless pattern combinations), it is not surprising that they are the most expensive surfaces to buy.

The cheapest alternative to grass is rough-chopped bark, which provides a soft landing surface for wobbly toddlers and can be used as a good temporary measure. Grit is another fairly economical material that is useful for uneven surfaces, although it is definitely not child-friendly. There are many reconstituted-stone paving products on the market: some of these imitations are so good that they are often difficult to distinguish from the real thing.

Two different surfaces used together in a small space can help to make an otherwise flat area far more interesting. Cobblestones mix particularly well, and can be used to create both unusual textures and eye-catching geometric patterns. Concrete slabs look extremely hard and unwelcoming on their own but, when mixed with areas of brick or cobbles, become much more interesting. Add a few plants here and there, and suddenly you have a garden.

PLANTINGS

Keep flower beds to the sides of the garden, in order to leave an uncluttered space that is as large as possible in the centre. Raised beds make maximum use of space and, although they are expensive to build, will pay dividends by providing superb growing space that can be gardened and kept looking good with the minimum of maintenance.

In a small garden every plant has to earn its keep by providing interest for much of the year, whether in the form of leaf shape, flowers, fruit or coloured stems. A basis of evergreen shrubs selected for year-round colour will give a backbone to the garden. Then add bulbs, along with summer-bedding and herbaceous plants for individual splashes of colour or architectural shapes.

Select shrubs that either do not grow too large, or can be regularly pruned. For example, many of the coloured-stemmed dogwood species naturally grow too large, but they can be cut back to ground level every spring for a fresh crop of shoots each year. Camellias eventually make large, spreading bushes, but they grow slowly and are well worth the space in any garden.

No garden should be without one or two architectural plants, which provide striking accents with their dramatic contrast in foliage. In areas that experience mild winters, choose the large, sword-shaped leaves of New Zealand flax (*Phormium tenax*) or the stiffer, more formal leaves of the

ABOVE: All vertical surfaces can be put to good use in a small garden. Roses add scent and colour.

cabbage palm (*Cordyline australis*). For colder areas, these two subjects make ideal container plants which can be moved inside for the worst of the weather. Flag irises are a tougher alternative and, although the leaves will die down over the winter, there is the bonus of their wonderful, almost architectural flowers in early summer.

Most trees grow much too large for small gardens, though you may have space for a silver birch or crab apple such as *Malus* 'John Downie', both of which are elegant, interesting trees for most of the year. Other possibilities are fruit trees such as apples or peaches which have been grown on dwarfing rootstocks; these should be readily available from good garden centres.

WALLS AND TRELLISES

Incorporate all vertical surfaces into the garden by clothing them with plants. If you do not have any such surfaces, create them by putting up fences, trellises and pergolas.

Trellises do not have to be completely covered in plants to look good, and can be a feature in their own right if painted in unusual or bright colours. Sky-blue wood against bright green leaves makes a stunning combination. Some plants, such as ivy and the climbing hydrangea (*Hydrangea petiolaris*), will climb unaided up a sheer wall; others, such as clematis, wisteria and honeysuckle need to cling to a trellis or to a set of wires. A whole group of plants such as ceanothus, climbing roses and flowering quince (*Chaenomeles speciosa*) can be trained against a wall, although they are not strictly climbers.

Hanging baskets or wall-mounted containers break up bare surfaces and provide an accent of colour, but they do need the constant attention of watering and feeding during the summer. To provide extra height and to add another dimension to the garden, grow plants up wigwams made of bamboo canes or rustic hazel twigs: these are ideal for a crop of runner beans, climbing nasturtiums or fragrant sweet peas. Free-standing trellis can also be used for instant screening and for creating secret play areas, making the garden seem larger by devising a series of rooms.

A mirror placed strategically in the garden is a clever ploy for a small area, often creating the illusion of twice as much space. Children will love the trick, but watch out for birds, which are easily fooled by the illusion and may fly into it, damaging their wings.

CHILD'S PLAY

In even the smallest of gardens there is plenty of scope for keeping children interested and active. An old lorry or tractor tyre, treated with bright paint, takes up little space and can be used first as a sandpit and then for a child's garden. A "real" miniature garden can be created in a large box or gravel tray using alpine plants, miniature roses and home-made wooden furniture. A bubble fountain is completely safe and always a great attraction. It also functions as a bird bath, and can be used to complement bird feeders positioned to be viewed from a window.

BELOW: A gravel tray makes a miniature garden to grow a small collection of alpine plants. Keep it in a sheltered corner and water regularly.

STORING TOYS AND EQUIPMENT

If there is one thing that will upset a relaxing afternoon in the garden, it is falling over children's toys left lying about. Hopefully, you will already have a place organised for storing tools, but the question is how to squeeze the new bicycles, scooters and buckets and spades that arrive every year into what may already be a limited space. As tools are generally an expensive investment and make dangerous playthings, they should ideally have their own storage area that can be kept safely locked. Inevitably, however, you will end up piling everything in the garden shed, if you have room for one: tools, garden furniture, bulky outdoor toys, bikes and a mass of other things.

A standard shed is usually bought as a prefabricated kit with the parts ready to put together. The main items of the kit will be the sturdy frame timbers, the panels to make up the sides and probably plywood sheets for the roof. It is advisable to erect the shed on a level concrete base or on firmly bedded paving stones. This is mainly to prevent the wood from rotting on damp ground. Most garden sheds are made of wood that has been treated with a non-toxic preservative, which will need to be re-applied at intervals. Some preservatives are poisonous to plants, so if you plan to grow plants against the shed or in close proximity to it, check the details of the preservative carefully.

As a new shed can be rather an eyesore, help to blend it in with the rest of the garden by painting it dark brown, green or black – the least obtrusive colours – or camouflage it with plants. For the latter option, use free-standing panels or screw a trellis to wooden blocks so that both this and the climbers can be lifted away from the shed when it needs to be treated with more preservative. Avoid plants that rapidly form a great mattress-like growth; instead, choose species with a controlled growth that benefits from being pruned from time to time, such as Trumpet creeper (*Campsis radicans*) or perhaps a climbing rose whose thorns will prevent the roof of the shed becoming a jumping board for nimble children.

A lean-to built against a wall or fence is a less elaborate and cheaper way of providing storage for tools and toys. Acrylic or PVC sheets can be used for the roofing. The main drawback of an open-structured lean-to is that it cannot be locked, although you could bolt or bracket tools to the wall and install a lockable cupboard under the lean-to for smaller or more valuable tools. Bikes can be lifted on to sturdy hooks to be tidily suspended, one above the other, against the wall.

Smaller still, a storage cupboard from the house can be adapted for outdoor use. However, this will offer little in the way of security unless it is made of metal and bolted to a solid wall, or made of wood and securely wall-mounted.

LEFT: *New sheds stick out like a sore thumb, but climbing plants can be trained to grow up and over them.*

OPPOSITE: *A free-standing trellis covered with plants creates a useful space for storing outdoor equipment.*

CHAPTER THREE

BALCONIES AND ROOF GARDENS

A fun, high-level garden can be created from either a balcony or a roof space, provided that care is taken over the basic construction at the initial planning stage. The main priority with a garden of this kind – especially when it will be used by children of any age – is that of safety. Any balcony or roof garden must be surrounded by a strong barrier that is tall enough to prevent a child from falling accidentally. All the fixtures used in the balcony must also be strong and secure. Even if these security measures have been undertaken and then double-checked, never leave children to play unsupervised on a balcony or roof space.

Above: Berberis thunbergii 'Atropurpurea Nana' is a good plant for balconies and roof gardens as it can withstand dry, exposed conditions.

Opposite: The ideal family balcony or roof garden is a place designed for sitting, playing and gardening. It should improve the quality of family life and brighten up the appearance of the building.

PLANTING SUGGESTIONS

High-level gardens are usually exposed to stronger winds than those at ground level because streets tend to act as wind tunnels, causing draughts to eddy up and round the buildings. Young plants are particularly vulnerable, so provide protection for them with wooden or plastic screens or wind shields. As the plants become established, they will provide protection for future plantings. Choose plants that are able to withstand dry, exposed conditions, such as *Berberis thunbergii* 'Atropurpurea Nana', *Hypericum* 'Hidcote' and

the blue grass *Festuca glauca* which makes a useful edging plant for beds and containers. Hardy Mediterranean plants also adapt well to exposed sites. Try the dwarf broom *Cytisus* x *kewensis*, a pale yellow bush with arching stems, *Genista lydia*, and catmint *Nepeta* x *faassenii*. Avoid plants with large leaves as they could blow over or tear in the wind.

A balcony garden can be used to frame or to obscure a view. It can be used for growing kitchen herbs, or as the "great outdoors" for all the family. You may find that a single line of pots or window boxes fills the balcony space, but remember that the plants used can benefit the interior as well as decorating the outside of the building. Traditionally, geraniums with scented leaves were grown in window boxes and on balconies to discourage flies from entering the house.

Hanging baskets filled with seasonal plants look colourful against walls and windows. Plant up a basket as a flowering fountain of mixed colour, or – for something popular with children – as an alpine basket or a miniature garden.

Birds, especially pigeons, can be a pest in high gardens. Sheer numbers cause damage through their acidic droppings, but sometimes it is the behaviour of just a few birds that causes problems. They may even decide to use window boxes as nesting sites, presenting the gardener with the dilemma of whether to sacrifice nest and eggs or prized young plants. If this is a potential problem, try threading dark cotton between the plants. Other pigeon scarers include the use of fine netting, glinting flags of tinsel or aluminium foil, scarecrows or anti-pigeon paint daubed on walls and balustrades.

LEFT: *Herbs grow well in containers and make useful and decorative additions to balcony areas. This window box has been linked up to an automatic watering system.*

OPPOSITE: *Here, wooden screens provide protection for the plants from the wind.*

MAKING SAFE AND SECURE

The main features that need careful examination before a roof garden or a balcony can be safe, secure and successful are those that will prevent you and your family from falling either *through* or *off* the garden. Be aware of the weight capacity of the roof or balcony, to stop you falling *through* it, and the strength of the enclosing railing or

BELOW: Safety does not have to mean ugly, prison-like bars. The strong, well-constructed trellis on this roof garden is a useful extravagance which is integral to the overall design.

balustrade to stop you falling *off*. Roofs and balconies are mostly designed to accept certain weights, and you can reckon on approximately 13kg per square metre (30lb per sq ft). This can be increased if you concentrate the weight in the corners and along the edges, and use lightweight pots or containers for the plantings. However, if you are in any doubt at all, you must consult a surveyor.

The materials used for surfacing the garden should be non-slip: this is especially important if the garden is at a high level and for wet conditions. As ceramic and concrete tiles are heavy, consider synthetic path matting. Even synthetic grass can look effective and provide a comfortable crawling surface for a toddler. Wooden decking is lightweight and, if it is laid across the garden, will help to spread the weight of pots or containers and allow water to drain away. Puddles of water can be slippery, so keep all drains clear and clean, and avoid blocking drainage with garden features such as pots and planters. You can buy small plastic or terracotta "feet" for planters and pots to allow free drainage beneath them.

You also need to take into consideration any danger to people below from dropped or blown objects, as well as the security of the site to prevent access by unwanted visitors. Walls of brick or stone are the strongest type and will last for a long time, but they are also the heaviest and the most expensive. Cost and weight can be reduced by using single-thickness, open brickwork, honeycombed with openings. While they let through light and air, unfortunately they also provide hand and foot holds for climbing.

Less costly than walls, fences and screens can be made of wood or woven willow stems, or even metal chain-link. Wooden fencing, trellising or screens could be the most effective solution, allowing you to change arrangements by removing or lowering the panels as children grow. Wooden fencing planks or trellis battens should be vertical and set close together to prevent children from climbing over them.

Above: A child-proof barrier leading to a balcony or roof space is a wise precaution, and an added security measure to keep unwanted visitors out.

All fences, screens and trellis panels must be firmly secured to prevent high winds from lifting or blowing them off the balcony or roof. Bear in mind that the wind resistance of an open screen or trellis will increase when it is covered with plants. Metal clamps can be used to fix trellis or screens to vertical drainpipes, but these devices may require some skill with a drill, and you may need to consult an expert.

Where metal railings and balustrades are firmly fixed to the building, children obviously need to be discouraged from the challenge of climbing and balancing on them. Window boxes fixed inside the top edge of railings will usually deter all but the most determined from climbing, especially if the plants hang inwards, on to the balcony. Make sure that such boxes are fixed very securely with strong brackets and wire, to prevent broken toes. A length of trellis fixed above a railing may act as a further deterrent both for climbing escapees and for potential invaders, particularly if the trellis is flexible and not too strong so that it bends towards the climber when it is pulled. Climbing or wall plants tied into the trellis such as *Euonymus fortunei* and *Jasminum nudiflorum* can have the same deterrent effect, but for the ultimate spiny repellent try a thorny pyracantha or a climbing rose.

Below: Metal railings reinforced with mesh are improved in appearance and security by the addition of sections of trellis fencing.

MAKING THE MOST OF AVAILABLE SPACE

Space for both planting and playing is usually limited in high-level gardens, so make the most of the available area with a careful choice of containers and planting design. Develop variation by establishing a backbone of structural plants, including some small trees and shrubs, and then provide seasonal colour and focus with herbaceous and flowering plants that can be changed and moved about as desired. Plant bulbs such as daffodils below other plants in pots and containers to push through and surprise you with spring colour. Lilies can be grown very successfully in pots, but do need more space than most bulbs.

To encourage children to enjoy and participate, the plants could include some edible ones suited to container growing, such as apple or pear trees, or, for more sheltered locations, peaches, oranges and figs. Strawberries can be grown in pots and hanging baskets, or as cascades in special strawberry-tower pots. A variety of vegetables including aubergines, French and runner beans, tomatoes, lettuces and radishes can all be produced in pots, grow-bags and other containers.

Climbers and wall plants can provide an amazing range of colours and textures in a limited space. They can be grown as a free-standing screen on wires, against a wall or trellis support, or even as a tent for shade and playing in. The site features and aspect are particularly important when choosing climbers or wall plants as these plants will probably be left in place while others are changed for seasonal variation.

For a landscaped effect, use big, lightweight, straight-sided containers in which you can group plants together, avoiding spot-planting. Clustering the pots will also create a favourable microclimate, giving the plants wind protection and increased humidity, leaving more space for the family. Big containers also need less watering.

OPPOSITE: *The planting area has been maximised by growing climbers, using pots and installing raised beds.*

Setting mirrors or reflective surfaces among the plants can create an illusion of more space and help to lighten up dark corners. And the use of well-positioned lighting can have a positive effect on the adjacent room, integrating the two areas more effectively, and increasing the sense of space.

Improvise a children's play area. Make a sandpit from an old lorry or tractor tyre, and help to create a woodland dell for mini-beasts and fairies from a second tyre, or from a rustic wooden crate filled with bark chips and planted with wild plants. Balconies can be as much fun as real gardens.

BELOW: *Raised beds are an alternative to containers for gardening in places where there is no soil. They allow a large number of plants in the minimum of space. The plants are also easier to maintain, requiring less watering and feeding, and are at a convenient height for weeding.*

HANGING BASKETS

Hanging baskets are the easiest way of brightening up an outside wall, and are a must when space is at a premium. They look most colourful in summer, and in winter can be planted up with small evergreens, heathers, winter-

RIGHT: Hanging baskets must be very firmly attached to the wall as they are extremely heavy when the soil is wet.

BELOW: Hanging baskets make an instant feature to brighten up walls and any vertical surfaces. They are easy to plant but require diligent watering, feeding and dead-heading to achieve long-lasting results.

flowering pansies and trailing ivies. Under-planted with a range of small bulbs, a winter basket will really cheer you up on a cold, dull day.

There are many different types, sizes and shapes of basket from which to choose, the most traditional being constructed from a wire frame; this may then be lined with plastic, foam, cardboard or coconut fibre. A thick layer of moss used to be the most popular liner for hanging baskets but, with the growing awareness of conservation issues, most people now think that sphagnum moss looks much more attractive.

Avoid very small containers, as these are difficult to keep well-watered during the summer. However, before you rush out to start planting up a basket, consider how you are going to hang it. A large, wet basket is extremely heavy, and will need a strong wall and special metal bracket to support it. It is also important to have easy access for watering, as during a long, hot summer a hanging basket will need watering twice a day. A bracket incorporating a spring-loaded suspension device that allows the basket to be raised and lowered for watering is very useful. Water-retaining gels are also worth using: these help to conserve water by forming minute water reservoirs on which the plants' roots can draw.

PLANTING UP A BASKET

1 Stand the basket on a pot or bucket to make it easier to work on, and then line the basket with a piece of black plastic or with a specially constructed liner made of foam, cardboard or coconut fibre.

2 Following the maker's instructions, mix a water-retaining gel into a multi-purpose compost. Place a shallow layer of compost in the basket, then add a saucer or circle of plastic to prevent water from draining straight through.

3 Start planting by poking seedlings or small pot-grown plants through the liner and into the compost. Work from the bottom upwards, and add more compost as you plant.

4 Put larger trailing plants in the final layer. For summer colour, use lobelia, geraniums and helichrysum; or plant autumn, winter and spring baskets with bulbs beneath ivies and heathers.

5 Water it well, then hang the basket up in your chosen position. Be sure to keep the compost moist, because most composts are difficult to re-wet once they have dried out.

CHAPTER FOUR

COMMON PROBLEMS IN THE GARDEN

The wonderful thing about spring is that both garden and gardener are full of hope and expectation. Everything is set to grow, flower and fruit to perfection. That is, before anything goes wrong. Later in the year, the garden's  vulnerability becomes apparent with outbreaks of a bewildering variety of pests and diseases. Plants are more prone to attack when they are under stress due to lack of water, incorrect nutrition or unsuitable growing conditions. A plant that is growing well in an open and well-cultivated soil containing plenty of organic matter is likely to outgrow or be resistant to many problems. The trouble with using chemicals to combat pests is that they often wipe out the helpful insects as well as the bad ones (as well as being potentially poisonous and allergy-triggering), but there may well be other options open to you.

ABOVE: In a family garden, mature trees and robust pest-free plants provide an inviting sheltered bower for young children to play in.

OPPOSITE: Dogs can cause havoc in the garden if they are allowed to run over flower beds. Vulnerable beds can be protected by a screen of rigid garden netting.

PESTS

Insect pests often do the most noticeable damage in the garden. They distort leaves and flowers by either eating the plants or by sucking out the juicy contents, and they can kill plants, often by transmitting diseases and viruses.

GARDEN PESTS
Aphids

Aphids are well known to all gardeners. They feed on plant sap, usually gathering in large numbers on young shoots, buds and the undersides of leaves, and cause damage by distorting growth and generally weakening the plant. They are also the prime offenders in spreading debilitating plant viruses. Aphids secrete an unsightly sticky substance called honeydew, which often covers plants and encourages the growth of black moulds. Ants feed on the sweet honeydew and seem to give the aphids some form of protection from their natural enemies: ladybirds and their larvae, and the larvae of lacewings and hoverflies.

If you have patience and you are not overly squeamish, use your fingers to squash aphids on the plant. An organic soft-soap spray will be reasonably effective, but for the best

ABOVE: Snails can make short work of any susceptible plants. The leaves of this hosta show signs of slug damage.

results you will need to use a spray that contains the chemical pirimicarb: this works specifically against aphids, leaving all the beneficial insects unharmed.

Whitefly

These tiny sap-sucking insects are common indoors and out. As they are attracted to anything yellow, sheets of yellow card smeared with thin grease (available in garden centres), and hung above the plants will help keep numbers down.

Slugs

Feeding at night on succulent young stems – often eating them at ground level so that the plants just topple over – slugs are the most infuriating of all pests. There is always a tell-tale slime trail left on the plants and the surrounding area. Large slugs feed mainly on plant material that is already dead; it is the small ones that are so destructive.

HEALTHY PLANTS

A happy, healthy plant will show resistance to many pests and diseases, and should be able to recover from most infestations if they do occur. The secret lies in the soil, which should be well cultivated so that it can hold air, food and water for the plants' roots. Organic matter is the secret ingredient that provides these conditions and makes a healthy soil. It may be difficult to obtain sufficiently large quantities of farmyard manure for this purpose, but every household can make garden compost and collect leaves to make nutritious leaf mould.

ABOVE: This hosta has been protected from slugs by a layer of coarsely chopped bark.

Keep the garden tidy, removing any rubbish and dead leaves lying on the soil surface that will provide dark, moist conditions where slugs can hide. During spring and autumn, keep an eagle eye out on warm, humid days, perhaps going out on a nocturnal patrol to pick slugs off the plants and drop them into a jar of paraffin or salty water. Susceptible plants such as hostas can be protected by surrounding them with sharp grit, coarsely chopped bark or lime, as slugs do not like sliding over any of these materials. Alternatively, grow these plants in pots.

A new biological control is now available by mail order; this consists of millions of microscopic eelworms which are released by mixing a sachet with water and watering the flower beds with it. The eelworms seek out and destroy the slugs quite effectively, but are quite expensive. Standard slug pellets pose a threat to other forms of wildlife in the food chain but, if you must use them, the least harmful type contain aluminium sulphate, which is shortlived in the environment. Hedgehogs, birds, frogs and ground beetles all eat slugs and should therefore be welcomed into the garden.

USING CHEMICALS SAFELY

Many chemicals are a potential hazard to all forms of life, and as such should only be used with caution as a last resort. Even though all products have been subjected to a long and costly testing procedure before they turn up on the shelves, nasty surprises and suspicious poisonings still occur occasionally. Take particular care when treating edible plants by scrupulously following all the manufacturer's directions concerning timing, concentration and the period before harvesting. Wise handling of chemicals in the garden – knowing when and what to use, and how often to use it – implies respect for the materials involved. Use all sprays on a calm day in the early evening when there are fewer beneficial insects (such as bees) about. Remember that chemical use should be combined with good gardening practice, and must never replace it.

Beetles

Most beetles are beneficial to gardeners, being natural predators of many pests. However, the unwanted beetles include some of the most destructive garden pests, which often do most damage in their larval stage. The asparagus beetle is very obvious with its black-and-yellow markings; both the larvae and adults feed on the leaves and shoots of the plant. Control these by picking them off by hand and destroying them. They are also susceptible to insecticides; spray in the early evening when there are fewer other insects about.

You may think the lily beetle a very attractive creature until you get to know it better. It is easy to recognise by its brick-red colour, and by the disgusting-looking larvae which resemble blobs of dirty jelly. Both the larvae and adults feed on the leaves and stems of lilies, and reproduce very quickly. Pick them off by hand and squash them.

Caterpillars

Caterpillars make short work of the plants they feed on. The apple maggot is the caterpillar of either the codling moth or the apple sawfly. Both insects lay their eggs in the developing fruit, so that the caterpillars eat away inside as the fruit swells. They are virtually impossible to control, so you will usually have to sacrifice a percentage of your crop every year.

HOUSE AND GREENHOUSE PESTS
Mealy bugs

Mealy bugs are small, sap-sucking insects that are protected by a dirty white, waxy coating. Control by brushing them with methylated spirits.

Red spider mites

Red spider mites are minute sap-sucking pests that can just be seen with the naked eye. Attacked leaves appear silvery where the plant cells have died, and in severe infestations the mites cling together, creating large sheets of webbing on the leaves. These pests are difficult to control because of their resistance to many chemicals. Pick off affected leaves and keep the air humid around the plant by regularly spraying it with water, as red spider mites do not like wet feet.

Scale insects

Scale insects have a protective shell, under which the insects live while feeding on sap. If possible, patiently rub them off with a damp cloth.

Vine weevil

This one is a real menace; you should learn to recognise it so that you can destroy it on sight. The ugly grubs live in

ABOVE: Dogs have a habit of trampling on flowers, so try and train them to keep off flower beds.

pots filled with compost, and feed on plant roots. Damage may first become apparent when you investigate, only to have the plant come away in your hands because all the roots have gone. A new biological control using nematodes is proving to be effective against this pest.

CATS AND DOGS

Cats unearth freshly sown seed, disturb young plants and leave droppings. Dog faeces left lying on lawns are a hazard. A bitch's urine can kill patches of grass, and male dogs tend to spray bushes, causing them to turn brown and die.

EMERGENCY AID

FOR INSECT BITES AND STINGS

If you are stung by an insect, use tweezers to remove the sting that is left in the skin. Rinse the area under cold running water. Antihistamine is good for soothing bites and stings. Seek medical advice if the pain does not subside after a few hours.

DISEASES

Plants suffer from some awful diseases such as mildew, canker, rot and blight, and once established there is often little chance of saving the plant. Prevention is better than cure, and clean growing conditions go a long way to stopping diseases from gaining a foothold in the first place. The majority seem mainly to attack fruit and vegetables, but there are some diseases common to the ornamental garden too.

Rose black spot

This is the most troublesome and common rose disease. Large black spots develop on the leaves, which prevents them from functioning properly and weakens the plant, often leading to defoliation. It spreads very quickly, so infected leaves should be removed as soon as they are noticed. Some roses are more prone to black spot than others, and in certain localities a susceptible variety will need regular spraying with a rose fungicide or sulphur. When buying roses, look out for varieties that are resistant to black spot.

VIRUSES

Symptoms are usually mottled leaves, general ill-health and unexplained distortions in leaves, stems or fruits. Tomatoes, cucumbers and their relatives such as marrows and courgettes are prone to viral diseases. As there is no cure, it is best to destroy plants to stop the disease spreading further. Plants may also suffer from other ailments such as bitterness, bolting and sometimes even blindness, but there is no point in losing sleep over these.

PLANT DISEASES

Plants are more susceptible to mildew if the soil is too dry; so try and keep it moist.

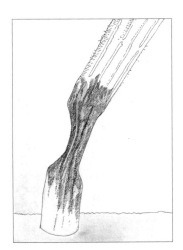

To prevent canker, avoid overwatering and keep water away from the base of the stem.

Petal blight spreads rapidly in wet weather. Cut off infected blooms and burn them.

Black spot on rose leaf is probably the most common disease of roses.

WEEDS

A weed is a plant that is growing in a place in which you do not want it. These are clever, adaptable plants that are often able to grow and reproduce extremely quickly in the most adverse conditions. Weeds are unwelcome because they compete with more desirable plants in the garden for light, water and food. It is important to keep them under control – and especially to prevent seed dispersal – because seeds are able to survive in the soil for more than 50 years, so that one year's seeding means many years' weeding.

It is easy to tell the difference between annual, shortlived weeds and perennial ones. Annuals pull out easily whereas perennials do not, so they should be treated differently. Annuals can be hoed, which means chopping them off at the roots so that they shrivel and die. Hoe regularly in sunny weather for time-saving, simple weeding. Perennial weeds, however, have a persistent root system to help them survive from year to year, and they must be dug out by hand, removing as much of the root as is possible. There are many thousands of plants that have become problem weeds, of which the following are a small selection.

LAWN WEEDS

Lawn weeds have a specially adapted low-growing habit, to help to protect them from the mower's blades. Many people like daisies and delicate drifts of pretty blue speedwells in a lawn, but other weeds are less welcome.

Plantain *(Plantago)*

This is identifiable by its clusters of leathery, ribbed leaves and erect spikes of tiny flowers. Use an old kitchen knife to cut out this weed from the lawn.

Dandelion *(Taraxacum officinale)*

This has a long tap root, and any small part that is left in the soil will grow into another plant. Dig it out carefully, using an old kitchen knife or a special weeding fork. Alternatively, dab each plant with a spot of selective weedkiller.

Clover *(Trifolium)*

This is often the only plant in the lawn to stay green during a long, hot summer; it thrives on lawns suffering from lack of water and nitrogen. Control this weed by applying a nitrogen-rich fertilizer in the spring, and by irrigating the lawn. Clover will also succumb to a selective weedkiller.

Moss

Moss is a symptom of a run-down lawn, but as it is so soft and green it can be appealing. Unless you discover the cause, using a moss-killer is a waste of time because it will only come back again. Moss is likely to appear in areas where there is poor drainage and poor nutrition, too much shade, or where the grass has been continually cut too short.

ANNUAL WEEDS

The following weeds are all relatively easy to keep under control by regular hoeing.

BELOW: Clover (Trifolium).

ABOVE: *Bindweed* (Calystegia sepium).

Ground elder *(Aegopodium podagraria)*

This appears mainly as a mass of leaves growing straight out of the ground. All the stems are below ground, creeping far and wide and able to produce new leaves all along their length. The stems are brittle, so careful digging out is necessary as every piece left behind can produce new plants.

Couch grass *(Agropyron repens)*

This vigorous grass has white, creeping stems that grow new shoots along their length. If the underground stems are cut up by soil cultivations they seem to develop twice as fast. Persistent digging up of the plant will eventually control it.

Bindweed *(Calystegia sepium)*

This has long, climbing stems that creep around other plants and can reach the top of a hedge in one season. It also has a mass of white and brittle underground stems. Every small piece that is left in the ground will grow into a new plant, making this weed extremely difficult to control.

Shepherd's purse *(Capsella bursa-pastoris)*

This forms a rosette of leaves, with a flowering stem about 45cm (18in) tall. The flowers are small and white, and the seed pods are triangular. When wet, the seeds are sticky and can be carried about on boots and garden tools. Up to 4,000 seeds can be produced by a single plant.

Japanese knotweed *(Polygonum japonicum)*

This grows to over 3m (10ft) tall with stems that look rather like a thick bamboo, flecked with purplish-red marks. It is an attractive plant with big leaves and clusters of cream-coloured flowers but it is difficult, if not impossible, to eradicate. All that can be done is to cut down all the shoots frequently; weedkillers do not seem to have much effect.

Dock *(Rumex crispus)*

This is a large weed that grows just about anywhere. It has a very tough tap root which can re-grow from the top 15cm (6in). It should never be allowed to set seed, as one plant can produce 30,000 seeds per year; these can last for up to 80 years in the soil. Dig out as much of the root as possible.

Groundsel *(Senecio vulgaris)*

This is a small weed, with ragged, coarsely toothed leaves. Each seed has a plume of hairs to catch the wind for dispersal; as the seeds are light, they can be carried over great distances.

Chickweed *(Stellaria media)*

This is a soft, limp, light green annual that can flower and ripen seed all year round. The seed can remain viable for a period of up to 40 years.

KEEPING PLANTS HEALTHY

All living things need food to grow and plants are no exception: they require a well-balanced diet, just as we do. Even though many plants have adapted to grow in all sorts of inhospitable environments, the majority that we grow in our gardens enjoy a rich, well-cultivated soil. The average soil normally contains enough plant food for initial plantings, but as you make heavier demands on flower beds, tubs and troughs it is important to replenish the food supply.

There are three main minerals required by plants: nitrogen, phosphorus and potassium (usually referred to by their chemical symbols – N, P and K). There are also a number of

BELOW: This compost area has been cleverly placed so that it is shielded from the rest of the garden by a brick wall.

minerals called trace elements: these are needed only in minute quantities, but are just as vital to plant health. The best way to supply these foods is to add either farmyard manure, garden compost or leaf mould to the soil. These bulky materials not only supply nutrients but also condition the soil, creating a healthier environment for roots.

Horse manure is one of the finest soil conditioners; if there is a riding stable near you, befriend the operators. As with all fresh manures it should be left to rot down for at least three months before using, otherwise the rotting process removes valuable nitrogen from the soil. Every household should have its own compost bin: the contents are the equivalent of a three-course dinner for plants and soil.

The model shown opposite is extremely easy and quick to make. It is particularly suitable for first-time compost makers, and for small gardens. The container is so small that it can be discreetly positioned among shrubs and moved around the garden. In a larger garden, make three or four bins to dot around, so that there is always a batch of compost ready for use.

LEAVES

Leaves should be composted separately because they take longer to rot down (normally about two years). Pile them in a corner of the garden, or fill black plastic bags and store them out of the way. Some leaves work better than others: oak and beech are best, whereas those with waxy coatings, such as plane and sycamore, take much longer.

WORMERIES

A specially adapted container (bought or home-made) is used to house brandling or tiger worms which are available from fishing shops. They process kitchen waste such as vegetable peelings, and produce a very rich, fine compost that should be used sparingly. The worms work extremely hard to digest

MAKING A COMPOST BIN

1 Tie a piece of wire or plastic netting, approximately 1.5m (5ft) in length, to make a cylinder.

2 Thread five bamboo canes through the wire. These should be 20cm (8in) longer than the height of the bin.

3 Push the canes into the ground, making sure the canes are vertical and secure. Line the inner surfaces of the bin with a layer of newspaper.

4 Fill the bin with kitchen waste such as peelings, evenly mixed with garden clippings. Make a lid from cardboard covered with a plastic bag.

ABOVE: Be careful what you put in your compost bin. Avoid cooked food, tough weeds, evergreen leaves, sticks and tough stems.

a thin layer of organic material every few weeks, so it is a relatively slow process. Keep the wormery indoors or somewhere with protection from weather extremes.

FERTILIZERS

All fertilizers give the ratio of nitrogen, phosphorus and potassium on the container as N:P:K. As a general rule, nitrogen is for leafy growth, phosphorus for healthy roots and potassium for fruit and flowers.

Fertilizers are useful for topping up plant foods, especially if manure or garden compost is in short supply. A dressing with a general-purpose fertilizer at the start of the growing season will benefit beds and container plants, and is a vital ingredient in composts. Many fertilizers release plant foods slowly over time, and can be either organic or chemical. Summer displays in containers, such as window boxes and baskets, should be fed at least once a week with a liquid fertilizer high in potassium.

CHAPTER FIVE

YOUNG GARDENERS

Being inquisitive by nature, most children love gardening because there is so much to discover both above and below ground. They also enjoy using interesting tools and getting thoroughly dirty, and there is the reward of seeing colourful flowers and harvesting delicious food.

Children under six years of age enjoy play activities such as filling pots with compost, but need constant help and supervision for seed sowing and planting. When they are about six or seven years old they can accomplish many gardening tasks without too much help, and are capable of gardening quite happily on their own.

Many children go through a gardening phase when they are desperate to grow something; if encouraged, this can lay the foundation for a lifelong interest.

ABOVE: Gardening is not just for grown-ups. By encouraging children to garden you will increase their awareness of their environment.

OPPOSITE: Watering is a favourite with all ages, but is particularly suited to children under six who have difficulty managing other garden activities, such as planting.

CHILDREN'S GARDENS

When children ask for a garden of their own, it can be difficult to find a suitable spot that is sunny, fertile and weed-free. The quickest and most convenient solution is to start container-gardening with them. Containers are ideal for children because, although small, there is still plenty of scope and, most importantly, every chance of success. Good results can be expected because containers are filled with potting composts that supply quality conditions for cultivating most plants. They are also virtually weed-free, which means that no boring weeding has to be done before the fun starts. If the interest in gardening shrivels early on, containers have the advantage of being easily absorbed into the rest of the garden, replaced with something else or simply removed. The major disadvantages of containers are that they require regular watering (at least once, if not twice, a day in sunny weather) and feeding (once a week during the growing season). This is a big responsibility for a young child, and an adult will probably have to help out.

Choose large containers, as small ones will heat up and dry out quickly in the summer. Virtually anything can be grown in a container, from traditional plantings of bulbs and spring bedding plants followed by summer flowers, to a selection of vegetables and herbs.

Start children off with a large pot or window box each, and if this is successful, let them expand their container empire. A wooden half-barrel is a good-looking container that will be big enough for most budding young gardeners to grow whatever they want.

CONTAINER IDEAS

For a bulb and spring bedding display: wallflowers, white tulips, forget-me-nots, dwarf narcissi, hyacinths, pansies and muscari.

For summer flowers: marguerites, snapdragons, petunias, trailing fuchsia, trailing verbena, helichrysum, nasturtiums and lobelia.

For an edible garden: 1 staked cherry tomato plant, 1 courgette, carrots, beetroot, parsley, basil and chives.

For a butterfly garden: primroses, phlox, wallflowers, asters, sedum, aubrieta, lobelia, candy-tuft, rosemary, catmint and lavender.

ABOVE: A wooden barrel makes a perfect first-time garden.

Before planting a wooden tub, add some drainage holes to the bottom. Then line it with a sheet of plastic, also with drainage holes, to help protect the wood. Next, prop it up on some flat stones, enabling water to drain away freely. And finally fill the tub with potting compost.

EDIBLE GARDEN

There is a good selection of compact vegetable varieties that can be grown successfully outdoors in large containers, but to avoid overcrowding grow no more than three or four different types together. Beetroot, carrots, French beans, lettuces and radishes can be sown directly into the container. Others, such as courgettes and tomatoes, are better started off in pots or bought as small plants. Many herbs are compact, tasty and decorative.

BULB GARDEN

Bulbs are excellent for first gardening attempts because there is an embryo flower in each one just waiting to burst out once it is given water and soil to grow in. Tall daffodil and tulip species look out of place in containers, so choose dwarf types such as Narcissus 'February Gold' and 'Tête à Tête', and tulips that grow no more than 30cm (12in) tall. Crocuses and muscari are naturally small; hyacinths are taller but are still ideal. All these spring-flowering bulbs should be planted in the autumn. They look very effective when mixed with other flowering plants such as winter pansies and wallflowers.

SUMMER BEDDING

Once the bulbs have finished flowering, dig them up and plant them in a temporary pot or odd corner of the garden, where the leaves can die down naturally and feed up the bulbs for flowering next year. Then plant the barrel with flowers to provide colour all summer. Garden centres offer a vast choice of summer bedding plants; alternatively, many are easy to start off from seed indoors. Old favourites for reliability as well as length of flowering are geraniums and fuchsias (both upright and trailing types), marigolds (for their bright orange and yellow colours), petunias, which love the sun, impatiens, which are good for shady conditions, and lobelia and silver-leaved helichrysum to tumble over the edge.

BUTTERFLY GARDEN

Plant a mixture of spring and summer flowers to encourage a variety of butterflies to visit the garden. These can include permanent plantings of asters, aubrieta, forget-me-nots, lavender, phlox, and primroses around the edge, with annual fillers such as lobelia for extra colour.

ABOVE: This miniature garden established in a strong wooden box is already two years old and will last for more years with careful weeding and pruning.

MINIATURE GARDEN IN A BOX

Miniature gardens delight children of all ages. They are usually made in a seed tray and last for only a few days but, if a slightly deeper container such as a gravel tray or sturdy wooden box is used, normal plants can be grown and the project becomes much more exciting. If it is planned carefully, the garden can last for many years, needing only an annual sort out, much like any other garden. Choose slow-growing evergreen plants for year-round colour, with small leaves that look in proportion. Rooted cuttings of small shrubs such as box, holly and pieris create an evergreen backdrop, and can

be pruned to keep them small. Miniature roses play the part perfectly and are an absolute must; treat them in the same way as any bush rose, pruning back by about half in spring. Small-leaved ivies are invaluable for training on to trellises and screens, and small alpine plants such as sisyrinchium, sempervivum and saxifrage are easy to grow, have small leaves and put up a good display of flowers. Dwarf upright conifers make ideal small trees, moss can represent grass, and a pie dish makes a pond. As children become involved in this world, you will be amazed at their enthusiasm and how absorbed they become.

ALPINE GARDEN

An old sink or stone trough is the perfect setting for an alpine garden, and needs only a few plants to look effective. Drainage is the most important factor, so put a layer of gravel at the bottom, and make sure that water can drain freely through the plughole. Fill up with a general potting compost and grit, mixed half and half, firming it down well. Landscape with small stones and strategically placed plants, then finish with a layer of gravel on the surface.

There are many suitable slow-growing alpine plants, such as dwarf conifers, thrift (*Armeria maritima*), dwarf carnation (*Dianthus alpinus*), *Phlox douglasii*, saxifrage, violets, sisyrinchium and sempervivum.

CAR TYRES

A stack of car tyres can make a cheap and cheerful container. Painted in bold colours and planted with a mass of trailing plants spilling over the side, they can look very effective. Two tyres on top of each other give a good planting depth, but for variation in height make them as tall as you like. To reduce the quantity of compost required, stuff the side walls with old newspaper or pieces of polystyrene packing material. Almost anything can be planted in a container this size, from cheap and easy annual flowers grown from seed to a pumpkin plant allowed to sprawl to its heart's content.

GROW-BAGS

Grow-bags make an instant and convenient garden to put down anywhere, and will certainly provide results. Try growing a bumper crop of tomatoes.

BELOW: Old tyres that have been given a lick of paint make generous planters that are absolutely free.

ABOVE: This boy's family have all planted their own Christmas trees but this is only appropriate for a large garden as they are forest trees that grow quickly and will soon outgrow the space available in a small garden.

SETTING ASIDE A PATCH

Some children are happiest helping out in the real garden, but for many a patch of their own is important. Avoid disappointments by providing a decent bit of garden to give a fighting chance of success. If you have enough space, choose a sheltered site and prepare the ground by clearing it of weeds; either do this yourself or help with the hard work. Children will then be eager to start soil cultivation themselves, forking it over, adding manure or compost and a sprinkle of fertilizer (under supervision), and then raking it level.

TOOLS

There is a wide range of quality children's gardening tools available. The best are not just toys, but are sturdy and practical, as well as rather cute. The most useful tools for children are small buckets, a wheelbarrow, a broom, a rake and a pair of good gloves, but there are also many adult tools that children can manage quite well. A trowel and fork will get most use, but for serious soil work and digging large holes a standard border spade and fork are ideal, and are so useful that you will all be fighting over them.

The biggest problem with other tools, such as rakes, brooms and hoes, is the handle length, which is too long for full control although most children do manage. A small watering-can designed for houseplants is an important piece of equipment. Children love watering, and it is one of the basic gardening skills for them to learn. Other handy objects

BELOW: Children enjoy the responsibility of using adult tools and even potentially harmful implements such as secateurs can be used under supervision.

ABOVE: There is a range of children's gardening tools available and, although not essential, equipment such as this jolly red wheelbarrow make gardening fun.

are a ball of garden twine, plant labels (make your own from plastic yoghurt pots), a waterproof pencil and a gardening notebook or diary.

Set aside some old clothing and a pair of sturdy shoes for gardening, and bear in mind that soft shoes – including rubber boots – can be hazardous, especially when a child is using a border fork that could accidentally spike his or her toes. When not in use, tools should be put away or laid down safely, forks stuck upright into the soil, and rakes laid with their teeth facing downwards.

An important lesson for adults to learn is to let children get on by themselves once they have been shown what to do. You may well be surprised by how much children can accomplish and how forgiving many plants can be.

OPPOSITE: Watering is always a popular job, especially on warm summer days.

WHAT TO GROW

For gardening to be enjoyable for children it is important they get a good result fairly quickly, so plants should be chosen for speed of growth and reliability.

BEST FLOWERS

Cornflower *(Centaurea cyanus)* ○ ◐ ❁

Sky-blue is the original colour, but pinks, purples and whites are now available. Grow from seed sown in autumn or early spring, either outside in its final position or in small pots to be transplanted. Height 60cm (2ft) and spread 30cm (12in).

Cosmos *(Cosmea)* ○ ✳

This is an impressive plant that forms a large bush from seed in just three months. It has ferny foliage and daisy-like flowers which bloom from midsummer until the first frost. Start indoors, sowing in small pots. Height and spread 1m (3ft).

Bleeding heart/Dutchman's breeches/Fat lady in the bath *(Dicentra spectabilis)* ◐ ❁

This charming plant is easy to grow either in sun or shade.

It dies down over the winter but is one of the first plants to pop up in the spring, with fresh green shoots followed by unusual, heart-shaped, rose-red flowers with glistening white inner petals. It has many common names, and suits them all! Height 75cm(2½ft) and spread 50cm (20in).

Fuchsia *(Fuchsia)* ◐ ✳ ❁

This has exotic bell-shaped blooms that last for months on end; there are hundreds from which to choose, with either trailing or bushy habits. Look for hardy varieties, which have flowers that are just as spectacular as the more delicate types, but plant them deeply. Tender bedding varieties should be lifted at the end of summer and kept dry until they are ready to start growing again the following spring. Height and spread variable, 60cm (2ft)–1.5m (5ft).

Sunflower *(Helianthus annus)* ○ ✳ ❁

Sunflowers never fail to be a big hit and, although children always want a tall one, there are many different-sized and interesting varieties. Sow two seeds in spring, in a hole just a few centimetres (1–2in) deep and, once they have germinated, thin them down to one seedling. Be sure to choose a position where there is a stable structure for tying in the plant, just in case you grow a record-breaker. Height from 60cm (2ft)–3m (10ft) and spread 45cm (18in)–60cm (2ft).

Lavender *(Lavandula)* ○ ❁

Lavender is happiest in sunny, fairly dry conditions, and is another good subject for growing in pots and containers of various sizes. To dry the flowers for an indoor display, pick them just before they have fully opened and then hang them upside-down in a cool, airy place. Height and spread variable, from 60cm (2ft) to 1.2m (4ft).

LEFT: *Cosmos flower all through the summer.*

LEFT: Sweet-smelling roses make lasting impressions on childhood summers.

a nuisance. The common name derives from the yolk-yellow centre and white petal edges. Grow from seed sown in the ground or in pots, in autumn or early spring. Height 15cm (6in) and spread 10cm (4in).

Sweet pea *(Lathyrus odoratus)* ○ ❀

Soak the seeds overnight before sowing in order to soften the hard seed coat. Sow them outside once the weather has warmed up in spring, or earlier in pots with a little protection. The sweetly scented blooms must be picked every day for the best results – the more flowers you pick, the more will continue to grow. Height to 3m (10ft) and spread 30cm (1ft).

Rose *(Rosa)* ○ ❀

The rose is a rather special, long-lived plant that can be grown as a climber, bush or even as a tiny miniature that is tough enough to live outside. For minimum trouble, try to find a variety that is resistant to the rose disease known as black spot. Children are quite capable of pruning roses themselves, when equipped with a stout pair of gloves and trusted with a pair of secateurs. Prune back bush types by about a half to one-third in early spring, cutting just above an outward-facing bud. Height and spread variable.

Lamb's ears *(Stachys byzantina)* ○ ❀

Grown for its woolly-looking leaves that are covered with soft, silvery hairs, this perennial plant will survive outside in all but the coldest areas. Its low growing height and delicate texture provide good contrast to a range of other plants and flowers. Cut it back in spring for a new flush of furry leaves. Height 60cm (2ft) and spread 45cm (18in).

Lily *(Lilium)* ○ ◑ ✳ ❀

Lilies have exotic, often heavily scented blooms. Although easy to grow, they are stately plants of which any gardener will be proud. Planted in groups of three or more for best effect, they are ideal for pot culture. Choose only bulbs that have healthy, fat white roots and plant them as soon as they become available, either in autumn or spring. Height and spread about 90cm (3ft).

Poached-egg flower *(Limnanthes douglasii)* ○ ◑ ❀

You only have to grow this flower once to have it in the garden forever, but it is so delightful that it never becomes

TOP TEN FRUIT AND VEGETABLES
All appreciate full sun; size and hardiness varies with variety.

Runner beans
Runner beans look great in a flower bed, providing instant height and colourful flowers followed by an endless supply of juicy green beans. Once the danger of frosts has passed, make a wigwam using four or five long bamboo canes, and then plant two or three seeds at the bottom of each.

Potatoes
Home-grown potatoes taste superb fresh from the soil, and harvesting them is the best gardening job going – rather like searching for buried treasure. They can be grown successfully in large plant pots or even in dark-coloured, strong carrier bags. Half-fill the pot or bag (make drainage holes) with potting compost and plant three potatoes several centimetres (1–2in) deep. When they have grown about 15cm (6in) tall, fill up the top with potting compost. Keep well-watered, and harvest 10–12 weeks later. You can use potatoes from your vegetable rack for growing, but to be assured of a good crop it is better to buy special seed potatoes.

Lettuces
Available in a large variety of sizes, shapes, colours and textures, lettuces are fairly quick to grow. For containers, choose small varieties such as 'Little Gem' and 'Tom Thumb', or a loose-leaf type such as 'Lollo Rosso', from which you can pick a few leaves at a time. To prevent a lettuce glut, sow a few seeds at first and repeat this every two or three weeks through the summer.

Beetroot
Beetroot is a neat, attractive plant; some types have colourful red leaves and look good in flower beds or planted containers.

ABOVE: A runner-bean wigwam makes an attractive centrepiece in a flower bed.

Carrots
Carrots are one of the easiest and tastiest vegetables to grow in a fertile, deep soil. The feathery foliage does not take up much space and the bright orange roots can be eaten small and young, or left to grow bigger in the soil. Sow carrot seed very thinly in rows, to avoid having to thin the seedlings which will attract carrot fly, a serious pest whose larvae tunnel into the roots.

Jerusalem artichokes
With stems reaching 2m (6½ft) in just one growing season, this plant is almost too easy to grow. It is ideal for out-of-the-way corners, but needs to be kept under control. After

the plants have died down in the autumn, eat the underground tubers, or keep some stored for the winter.

Fruit trees

A fruit tree is something to plant for the future and, although some apple and pear varieties can start cropping within two or three years, with age they just get better. The ultimate for longevity is a mulberry tree *(Morus nigra)*. Your children will probably be teenagers before it starts fruiting, but as it can live for several centuries they will be the first of many to enjoy the delicious fruits that it produces.

Blackcurrants

Blackcurrants are greedy plants that enjoy huge helpings of horse manure or garden compost. Keep the fruit large by pruning every winter, simply cutting out a few of the oldest stems. For small and medium-sized gardens, 'Ben Sarek' is the most compact variety. Be sure to net the bushes at fruiting time, or you will have to compete with the birds.

Tomatoes

Tomatoes make a satisfying and interesting crop for children who are capable of simple tasks such as tying-in, watering, feeding and, of course, picking. The rewards are high, with regular supplies of fruit over a long period. Little cherry tomatoes are the sweetest, and usually the favourite, and are well-suited to planting in grow-bags. They need staking, and the side-shoots must be removed to leave one main stem. There are also varieties that make small bushes no more than 30cm (12in) tall, and others that have a trailing habit.

Strawberries

For a real taste of summer everyone loves strawberries, and luckily they are both cheap and easy to propagate and grow. Buy the first few plants from a garden centre or from a

specialist grower to ensure that they are free of viruses and diseases, then increase your collection. Runners are produced at the end of long stems during the summer, and these can be pegged down into small pots to make new plants. Replace your strawberry plants every few years, as they will start to lose vigour after this time.

BELOW: Picking fruit is one of the easiest garden tasks for young children, even if most of the fruit goes into their mouths rather than the basket!

INVOLVING YOUNG GARDENERS

To avoid early disappointments, keep a watch for common gardening problems. Watering is a popular job for children but needs practice to know when and how much to give. Younger gardeners may need help with weeding and dead-heading

WATERING

Although watering might at first seem straightforward, more plants die from over-watering than from any other problem,

BELOW: Take care when watering!

ABOVE: When planting, children tend to put too many plants in the available space because they do not anticipate how large the plants are going to grow. Encourage them to read the instructions on seed packets or the information that comes with bedding plants.

and applying water correctly requires some skill. Houseplants are the trickiest, and as a general rule should only be watered when the compost has started to dry out and the pot feels light. The heaviness of a pot is a good rule of thumb, and it is a useful exercise to get children to feel the difference in weight between two pots of equal size – one just watered and one dry. Whenever plants are watered they should be wetted thoroughly – never just given a light sprinkle. The most crucial times for watering are after seed sowing and planting.

To avoid disturbing small seeds that have been sown in containers, they should be watered from underneath. Stand the pots in a tray of water and leave them for a few minutes until the surface of the compost glistens with moisture and the pot feels heavy. It is not necessary to water seeds sown in flower beds outdoors, but nor does it do any harm. Plants that are wilting from lack of water can make an incredible recovery if you catch them in time, and you can almost see the leaves spring back to life as the cells fill up with water. However, the experience of wilting does weaken a plant and, if it happens several times, it will become more susceptible to pests and diseases.

OVER-CROWDING

Planting too close is a common fault with gardeners of all ages, and plants that have to compete for light become spindly and weak. When plants are small, it can be difficult to envisage their full size.

Seedlings of outdoor-sown plants, such as lettuce, beetroot and most annual flowers, have to be thinned while still small to make enough room between plants. The problem is compounded by the fact that they are also usually heavy-handed at seed sowing. Seedlings that have been thinned out rarely transplant well, so it is best to teach hard-heartedness, and to throw them away.

WEEDING

Children often enjoy weeding, at least for short periods of time. The common difficulty lies in recognising the weeds, particularly where many hardy annuals have self-seeded. To make things easier, sow seed in straight rows, and mark each row. Then you will at least know that everything that comes up between the rows is a weed.

DEAD-HEADING

The sole purpose in life for most plants is to produce seed for the next generation so, as soon as they have achieved this, they stop making flowers and concentrate their energy

ABOVE: When weeding, small children need supervision to make sure that they do not pull out healthy plants.

on leaves or, if they are annuals, they die. For a long flowering display, remove the flowers as they fade to prevent seed from setting and to trick the plant into producing more flowers. Dead-heading is extremely important in extending the life of all bedding plants, and is a useful job for children to learn.

CHAPTER SIX

PLANNING AND PLANTING

When you move into a new house you may inherit a mature garden or have to start from scratch. In this chapter, there are four plans for family gardens. These can be adapted to suit your own requirements. Remember that correct planting is one of the most important gardening jobs. The most common fault is

to dig too shallow a hole, leaving the rootball exposed and prone to drying out. Digging plant holes that are sufficiently deep should be well within the capabilities of most children, provided that the soil has been cultivated by forking over first, and that they are given a decent trowel. As it is often difficult to imagine quite how much space each plant needs, another common fault – made even by experienced gardeners – is to plant too close together. This will cramp the plants, impeding their proper development.

Above: Honeysuckle is a wonderful scented climber.

Opposite: Annuals are good plants for a family garden. There is a wide variety to choose from at garden centres, but to keep costs down, grow them from seed sown in the spring.

DESIGN AND PLANTING PLANS

The following designs are for four small gardens, and are intended to be a flexible source of inspirational ideas. Bear in mind that, just as all gardens vary in shape, size and conditions, so will the results that you can expect to achieve.

First of all, consider what you have and what natural features can be incorporated. You may have an old tree to accommodate, or mature shrubs that require only regenerative pruning to get them back into shape. Many shrubs that have become ugly and overgrown can be pruned back to about 30cm (12in) above the ground. This will produce a fresh crop of young, vigorous shoots. If you are unsure about what you have inherited in the garden, wait for one growing season to see what happens. Once you know what features you have that are worth saving, then you can plan around them and maintain a feeling of maturity in the garden.

An uncluttered area is essential for safe play, with flower beds kept to the sides of the lawn or patio. Island beds do not make sense for a young family, but do try to leave areas of mystery in the lawn and borders. Ideally, you want comfort, beauty and convenience, combined with excitement, entertainment and space for children. In small gardens it is the hard landscaping, such as the patio, paths and walls, that is most crucial and the most expensive element to consider.

Paths should have a width of at least 1m (3ft). They must follow the most direct route through the garden, or people will take shortcuts. A washing line or clothes drier can be difficult to site, as it needs an airy spot where it will not get caught up in plants, and should be close to the house. A washing line takes up more room while clothes are drying but can be put away when not in use. Once you have a good idea of what there is in the garden and how you hope to use it, photograph the garden from as many angles as possible. Include views from the house because, for most of the year, that is how you will see your garden. Then draw a plan to scale on graph paper, first placing existing features and then deciding what you want to hide and what you wish to add. Plan the hard landscaping carefully, as it will be in place for a long time. Consider the boundaries and create interesting flower beds with lists of plants, their positions and combinations. Give the jobs priority according to need, money and time. In each plan, if more than one plant is required, the number needed is given in brackets.

ABOVE AND OPPOSITE: A garden that is designed for the whole family is a place that is exciting and safe for children, and a pleasant setting for you to relax in. In this garden the climbing frame is carefully concealed in the trees, and the crossbar creates an interesting break between this area and the garden beyond. The rustic poles blend in well with the garden scenery.

GARDEN PLAN NO.1

A small garden for easy maintenance

This garden has a simple design that is functional and easy to maintain, creating what is virtually an outside room. There will be a substantial initial outlay on hard-landscaping materials, which are a crucial element in the design of all small gardens, but the costs could be staggered by paving the garden in sections rather than all at once.

There are two areas of raised bedding, one on either side of the patio. These should be constructed at a height of 45–60cm (18–24in), and built of brick, decorative walling blocks or railway sleepers. The long stretches of wall will need a supporting pier at approximately 1.7m (5½ft) intervals, projecting by at least half a brick. Although expensive to construct, raised beds are a blessing in a small garden as they make maximum use of the limited space, and are easy to maintain and keep looking good all year round. The generous rooting depth of this type of bed also provides ideal growing conditions for the majority of plants. To take full advantage of this, the beds should be packed full and any gaps filled with bedding plants and bulbs. On the whole, the selected plants will take care of themselves, except for the climbing rose which needs annual pruning, and the *Clematis* x *jackmanii* and hardy fuchsias which would need to be cut back in early spring.

A low trellis between the utility and play areas provides a feeling of privacy for children, and in the play area itself there is a flower border to tempt young gardeners into action. Grow a selection of easy vegetables, such as runner beans and salad crops, or fast-growing annual flowers, such as a stunning backdrop of majestic sunflowers. Coarse bark chippings would provide an attractive, economical surface for a play area. For added interest, they are now available in different colours. The utility area would work well with a gravel surface.

1 Euonymus fortunei *(3)*; 2 Cotoneaster horizontalis; 3 Ajuga reptans *(5)*; 4 Alchemilla mollis *(7)*; 5 Hedera *(2)*; 6 Polygonum affine *(5)*; 7 Hydrangea petiolaris; 8 *Camellia*; 9 *Fuchsias (hardy)*; 10 Campanula carpatica *(5)*; 11 Juniperus x media; 12 Stipa arundinacea; 13 Tradescantia virginiana *(5)*; 14 Chaenomeles speciosa; 15 Daphne x burkwoodii; 16 Aubrieta sempervirens *(7)*; 17 Potentilla fruticosa; 18 Hakenochloa macra 'Aureola'; 19 Iberis sempervirens; 20 Lavandula 'Hidcote' *(3)*; 21 *Climbing roses*; 22 Ceanothus thyrsiflorus repens; 23 Clematis x jackmanii; 24 *Purple sage*; 25 Rosmarinus 'Miss Jessop's Upright'; 26 Nepeta 'Six Hills Giant *(3)*; 27 Lathyrus odoratus 'Upright' *(12)*; 28 *Trailing nasturtiums (12)*; 29 *Fill gaps with herbs and bedding plants.*

GARDEN PLAN NO.2
A small town garden in a semi-formal style

Stylish yet versatile, this small garden is laid out in a semi-formal fashion to provide plenty of space for lush plantings. It is a plant lover's garden, made with compromises to accommodate the needs of children. The plantings are robust and quick-growing, requiring minimum maintenance, but as children grow older there is plenty of scope for replacing the initial choice with more delicate species or bedding plants. It is a garden designed to be used in all seasons, with a strong evergreen structure that gives shape throughout the year.

The patio and paths would look attractive in brick or York stone paving, which are affordable options because of the small area involved. Alternatively, use concrete, re-constituted stone or crazy paving. The ring-road path provides a circular route for small tricycles, and should be evenly laid. To protect the beds, substantial edging is required. A brick raised bed is ideal and would make good use of space; or you could use bricks on their sides or even log-roll edging.

The central circular feature is edged with the dwarf box *Buxus sempervirens* 'Suffruticosa', and should be given a focal point such as a statue, sundial, birdbath or fountain, surrounded by the ground-cover plant *Euphorbia amygdaloides robbiae*. This will be an attractive area for children playing imaginary games, and they can easily step over the dwarf-box edge. A bark surface would not look out of place, and could be replaced later by gravel. Conical obelisks shaped from common box, holly, yew or bay, and planted among the dwarf box, could be added in years to come. The sandpit is sited on the patio so that any spilled sand can be swept up. A raised edge would be ideal, providing child-sized seating.

The den is just big enough to make a camp, and need consist of no more than two logs for seats. The low trellises at the front give a sense of privacy. Children could plant nasturtium seeds at the base to cover the trellises in the summer. When the children have outgrown the den, a matching herb garden would suit the overall design.

1 Hedera 'Goldheart' with Clematis montana (2); 2 Sambucus racemosa 'Plumosa Aurea'; 3 Choisya ternata; 4 Hydrangea quercifolia; 5 Arundinaria murielae; 6 Lonicera japonica 'Aureoreticulata'; 7 Hedera 'Goldheart' (2); 8 Euphorbia wulfenii; 9 Euonymuous 'Emerald' and 'Gold' with bulbs (5); 10 Hypericum calycinum (5); 11 Foeniculum vulgare (3); 12 Phormium tenax; 13 Hydrangea petiolaris; 14 Vinca minor (6); 15 Humulus lupulus 'Aureus'; 16 Brunnera macrophylla (5); 17 Camellia; 18 Lonicera x americana; 19 Fuchsias (hardy); 20 Photinia x fraseri 'Red Robin'; 21 Heuchera micrantha 'Palace Purple' (5); 22 Sarcococca humilis (5) with Alchemilla mollis (7); 23 Fern (3); 24 Helianthus annus (5); 25 Vegetables; 26 Lavandula 'Hidcote' (5); 27 Hybrid tea rose; 28 Cistus; 29 Hosta 'Blue Moon' (3); 30 Viola labradorica (in gaps); 31 Iris germanica (5); 32 Iberis sempervirens (10); 33 Ceanothus 'Autumnal Blue'; 34 Cytisus 'Lena' (3); 35 Dwarf Buxus (40); 36 Stachys lanata (5); 37 Buxus.

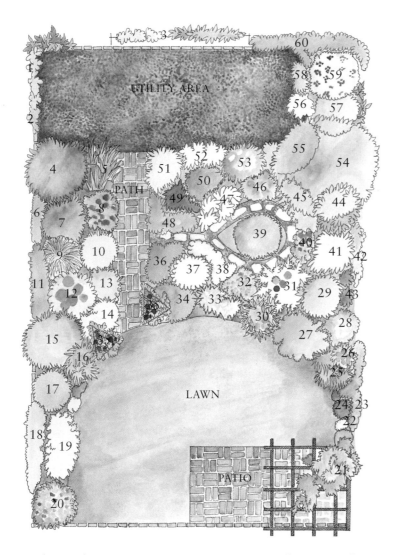

GARDEN PLAN NO.3

A family garden for a sunny site

This garden is both functional and attractive. The patio is covered with a trellis adorned by climbers to provide shade. A wisteria would be a good choice but would need regular pruning, especially in the early years. You can choose an easier plant such as *Lonicera* x *americana*.

The curved lawn is not huge, but creates a play area. The utility area is a versatile space for the washing line, compost bins and storage, or could be used as a play area. Later on it would be easy to make this into a flower bed or even a vegetable patch. The path makes a useful cycle track. The secret garden is tiny, but still large enough to grow a small willow that will serve as a den. Alternatively, children could plant a patch of annuals or make a bubble fountain.

The small tree, a snowy mespilus (*Amelanchier lamarckii*), provides height. This species can make either a small tree or a large shrub, so for a specimen tree it is important to select a plant with a main stem of at least 1.2m (4ft) before the branches start. The eventual height is about 4.5–6m (13½–18ft). This garden is packed with plants but still maintains a light and open feel, mixing grey-leaved sun lovers with pale pinks and blues. The plantings provide good colour and flowering displays, but are also tough.

1 Hedera; 2 Clematis montana; 3 Lonicera japonica *'Halliana' (on trellis)*; 4 Photinia *x* fraseri *'Red Robin'*; 5 Bearded irises *(5)*; 6 Humulus lupulus *'Aureus' (on wall)*; 7 Weigela *'Bristol Ruby'*; 8 Aster amellus *(5)*; 9 Miscanthus sinensis; 10 Hebe *'Midsummer Beauty'*; 11 Chaenomeles speciosa; 12 Hydrangea serrata *'Grayswood'*; 13 Artemisia *'Powis Castle'*; 14 Spiraea *'Gold Mound' (3)*; 15 Choisya ternata; 16 Pleioblastus auricoma; 17 Cotinus coggygria *'Royal Purple' with* Iberis sempervirens; 18 Ceanothus *'Autumnal Blue'*; 19 Liriope spicata *(7) and* Alchemilla mollis; 20 Fuchsia *'Mrs Popple'*; 21 Wisteria *(on trellis)*; 22 Daphne odora *'Aureo-marginata'*; 23 Climbing rose; 24 *Bedding plants to fill gaps*; 25 Festuca glauca *(7)*; 26 Phlox; 27 Ceanothus repens; 28 Viburnum bodnantense; 29 Taxus baccata *'Fastigiata Robusta'*; 30 Cistus *'Silver Pink'*; 31 Globe artichoke *(3)*; 32 Rosa floribunda *'The Fairy'*; 33 Physo-stegia virginiana *(5)*; 34 Heuchera *'Palace Purple'*; 35 Trellis obelisks with *climbing roses or clematis*; 36 Hebe pinguifolia *'Pagei' (5)*; 37 Phlomis fruticosa; 38 Achillea *'Moonshine' (5)*; 39 Salix caprea *'Kilmarnock'*; 40 Geranium sylvaticum *'Album' (3)*; 41 Lavatera *'Barnsley'*; 42 *Clematis with* digitalis *in the gaps*; 43 Euonymus fortunei *'Silver Queen'*; 44 *Rhododendron*; 45 Dicentra spectabilis *(3)*; 46 Bergenia cordifolia *(5)*; 47 Stachys byzantina; 48 Lavandula *'Hidcote'*; 49 Monarda didyma; 50 Taxus baccata; 51 Cistus *x* purpureus; 52 Sedum spectabile *(3)*; 53 Phila-delphus *'Belle Etoile'*; 54 Amelanchier lamarckii; 55 Helleborus orientalis *(3)*; 56 Hypericum *'Hidcote' (5)*; 57 Mahonia aquifolium *(3)*; 58 Vinca minor *(3)*; 59 Cotoneaster *'Hybridus Pendulus'*; 60 Hydrangea petiolaris.

GARDEN PLAN NO.4

A small- to medium-sized family garden

With a backdrop of evergreen and deciduous shrubs, punctuated by perennial flowering plants, this garden allows for plenty of lawn space where the children will be able to play. The plants need little maintenance, but the lawn will require regular attention. The solid timber post swing could later be converted into a flower-covered arbour.

The patio provides a seating area, as well as space for a small tyre sandpit or for a child's container garden. An architectural plant such as the sword-shaped leaves of New Zealand flax (*Phormium tenax*), planted in a large pot, adds a dramatic flourish to the patio and requires little attention. The handsome large-leaved tree, *Magnolia grandiflora*, has shiny evergreen leaves and is best grown as a wall shrub. It is fast-growing, with white, saucer-shaped, scented flowers in the summer. The lean-to provides parking space for bikes, and is cheap to build using a Perspex roof. The shrub border to the left of the path has several large shrubs to form a solid block of interest. Fill any gaps, while waiting for the shrubs to mature, with spring bulbs and ground-cover plants such as periwinkle (*Vinca minor*) and *Ajuga reptans*.

The shed is softened by the loose growth of kerria and forsythia, and by the evergreen backdrop of ivy behind. The *Prunus avium* is a wild cherry tree. Underplanted with a carpet of spring flowers, and bordered by hollies and the Guelder rose (*Viburnum opulus*), it creates a woodland feel that can be encouraged with the use of bird-feeders, birdbaths and piles of rotting logs for insect activity.

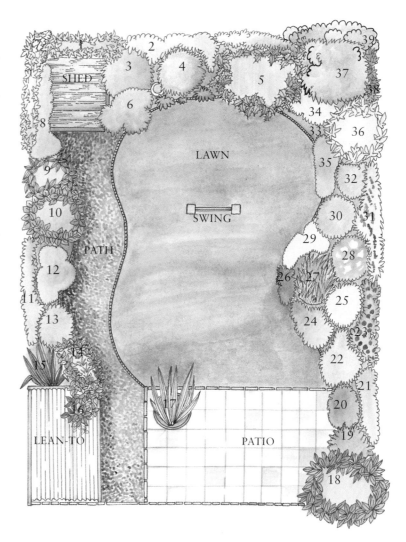

1 Hedera *with* Lonicera; 2 *Rosa*; 3 *Forsythia*; 4 Buddleia globosa; 5 Ilex *(3)*; 6 Skimmia *'Kew Green' (3)*; 7 Hedera; 8 Kerria japonica; 9 Viburnum tinus *'Eve Price'*; 10 Corylus maxima *'Purpurea'*; 11 Hydrangea petiolaris; 12 Berberis thunbergii *'Erecta' (3)*; 13 Camellia; 14 Liriope muscari *(7)*; 15 Phormium tenax *'Red Robin'*; 16 Clematis montana *'alba'(to grow over roof)*; 17 Phormium *(in pot)*; 18 Magnolia grandiflora; 19 Rosmarinus *'Miss Jessop's Upright'* ; 20 Lavandula *'Hidcote' (5)*; 21 Lonicera *x* purpusii; 22 Sarcococca humilis *(3)*; 23 *Climbing rose*; 24 Heuchera *(5)*; 25 Hebe; 26 *Flag iris (5)*; 27 Centaurea *(5)*; 28 Philadelphus *'Belle Etoile'*; 29 Berberis thunbergii *'Atropurpurea Nana' (3)*; 30 Rosa rubrifolia; 31 Buddleia *'Lochinch'*; 32 Rosa rubrifolia; 33 Ajuga reptans *(to fill any gaps)*; 34 Helleborus orientalis *(3)*; 35 Brunnera macrophylla *(7)*; 36 Viburnum opulus; 37 *Ground cover of* Polygonatum multiflorum *(7)*, Primula vulgaris *(7) and* Lamium galeobdolon *(7)*; 38 Hedera; 39 Prunus avium.

SHORT-STAY GARDENS

Short-stay gardens pose certain problems, among which is the decision of which plants to take with you when you go, and which to leave behind. Many plants can be moved, either entirely or as cuttings, divisions or seeds.

With a short-term garden, you should spend time at the start thinking about the plants, the design of the garden and the choice of surfacing and ground-cover plants, so that you do not spend an inappropriate amount of time or money on something you will only enjoy for a brief period.

Obviously, you will be influenced by the garden with which you start, and by whether it is a bare open space, a simple patch of grass or a partial garden with some structure. If you start with a lawn or paved garden, there is little point in changing this and you can concentrate instead on the plants. However, if you start with a bare patch, then grass is among the least expensive of surfacing options for the open stretches, but will of course take time to develop from seed; turf is very much quicker. More immediate surfacing can be created with bark chips or gravel, laid on woven, nylon sheets through which water will drain. Gravel is more expensive than bark, but presents a wider choice of colour and particle size.

Annual plants are the cheapest and easiest way of brightening up a short-stay garden. Sow them yourself or use seasonal plants bought from a local garden centre to fill out beds and boxes, all of which can be moved with you. You can also grow vegetables and herbs in the same way.

When selecting other plants, it helps to know their growing habit. Shrubs or trees that are often slow-growing and expensive, such as rhododendrons, conifers and even holly, can be grown in pots sunk into soil or stood on the edges of paving or paths. Investment in large pots can be avoided for many trees and shrubs if you cut around and under the roots with a sharp spade once a year. This will encourage the development of young feeding roots near the rootball, ready for when it is dug up. Alternatively, you can plant into root bags – special thick fibre bags that prevent extensive growth of large roots. Root bags can be bought at large garden centres, and allow shrubs and trees to be moved without the work of undercutting.

Pots can also be used for climbers. For example, most clematis varieties can withstand hard pruning and can be cut back before being moved. However, their roots prefer to be cool, so the pot should be kept shaded. Other climbers, such as the golden hop (*Humulus lupulus* 'Aureus'), are fast-growing, rampant climbers and, as they die back to the ground each year, can be easily moved out of season. Most woody wall plants can also be relocated if you have tied them to a trellis or to wires: simply cut them free, prune them back and then loosely tie up the stems.

A short-stay garden can be a challenge but also an inspiration. It provides the perfect opportunity to explore propagation techniques, enabling you to fill out the flower beds and to take something with you when you go.

LEFT AND OPPOSITE: *The use of bedding plants is the quickest and most effective way of making a splash of colour.*

PLANTING THE FOUNDATIONS

Although selecting the plants may be the final stage in planning a new garden layout, it is in many ways the most important and the most challenging of all, because it is the choice of plants that will bring your garden to life.

Many plants are easy to please and will grow in most conditions; others are more difficult. If you have obvious extremes in your garden – such as a very sunny, dry flower bed, or heavy soil – compile a checklist of plants that will do well in the different locations. One good way to obtain an idea of which types of plants are likely to thrive in your garden is to peer over the fences of gardens nearby.

Colour is usually the first plant attribute that springs to mind, but do not overlook the power of pure shape and texture. Varieties in foliage can be one of the richest visual aspects of garden plant life, with seasonal changes providing ongoing interest throughout the year, and you should remember that green is a colour too.

In every garden design there should be focal points, which may be trees, shrubs or man-made garden features. Combined with a selection of decorative and pretty plants, such as flowering shrubs and perennials, these will be set off to best effect against a background or skeleton of plants, such as evergreen shrubs and hedges, that provide year-round interest.

The longest-lived plants should be planned and planted first. Even when you are designing a garden on a tight budget, this means all the trees, shrubs, hedges and the slow-growing climbers that will form a permanent backbone, or structure, for the garden. Position these plants carefully, paying attention to their final size and allowing plenty of room between each one and the next permanent shrub. It is often possible to correct mistakes by moving plants with large rootballs (in the dormant season), but there is always a risk that they will not transplant successfully. Even if they do take well in their new location, this will set back their development by at least a year.

When positioning any plant, consider the height, shape, texture and colour of the leaves and flowers, and endeavour to create contrasts within different planting groups. Smaller plants should be in drifts and, as a general rule, odd numbers of either five or seven look the most natural. Plant groups slightly apart, but close enough to be good neighbours and to make an attractive wave of foliage. Fill in the gaps with inexpensive colour created by annual flowers such as nasturtiums and marigolds, which can be replaced easily and will not cause broken hearts if they become damaged.

ABOVE: Here are two gardens which are very similar in shape to the garden opposite, long and narrow, but these are more mature. In both cases the borders have been planted up as the children have got older, reducing the lawn area and adding interest to the overall design.

OPPOSITE: This simple design is perfect for a young family. It has a large, uncluttered lawn area for children's play, and the boundaries are secure. There are no flower beds yet, but when the time is right they will be easy to develop.

SHRUBS, BEDDING PLANTS AND PERENNIALS

The best time to plant is in spring or autumn when there should be plenty of rain to help the plants become established. Winter can be too cold and wet, and the summer too hot and dry.

BULBS

It is the depth of planting that is most important with bulbs. As a general rule, plant them with the tips of the bulbs about three times as deep as the length of the bulb. If in doubt, it is better to plant deep rather than shallow. To avoid straight rows and to create a more natural effect, throw a handful of bulbs on to the soil and plant them just where they fall.

TREES

The larger the garden, the more important it is that it should contain trees. Those that will be suitable for a domestic garden should have a small and compact habit of growth. Birch, crab apple and rowan are all suitable.

ABOVE: A mixed spring border brightens up a brick wall, with a fantastic flowering display of tulips, pansies and primroses.

HOW TO PLANT

1 Dig a hole just deeper than the plant roots. To check this, put the plant in position and place a stick across it.

2 Turn the pot upside-down and tap it sharply to free the rootball. Remove the pot and separate the lower roots.

3 Put the plant in the hole and cover over with soil, pressing it firmly around the roots. Water the plant generously.

PLANTING A TREE

1 Using a spade, dig a hole at least 10cm (4in) deeper than the pot depth.

2 Fork over the base of the hole and add a generous helping of manure.

3 Take the tree carefully out of its pot and place it in position.

4 Insert a short stake close to the roots and hammer it firmly in place. Once in position, the stake should come to just below the first branch.

5 Replace all the dug-out soil in the hole, firming it around the roots as you go. Fix two tree-ties, one near the bottom and the other at the top.

ABOVE: Finally, give the tree a soaking with water. After about three years, when the tree is well established, the stake can be removed.

INDESTRUCTIBLE PLANTS

Inevitably, you learn to accept damage limitation to garden plants when you raise a family. Apart from causing general wear and tear – such as compaction of flower beds and patchy, thin lawns – exuberant youngsters may break branches and snap stems. However, although it would be silly to position a prized plant on the edge of a well-used path or in the middle of a lawn, accidents occasionally happen and they are not worth worrying about unduly. To avoid heartache, do not grow plants with brittle, delicate stems that are likely to sulk if they are inadvertently disturbed or damaged. Plants such as Japanese maple (*Acer palmatum*), peonies and *Magnolia stellata* need cosseting and are plants for the future; others are more resilient and will look after themselves. The following plant suggestions are some of the most sturdy (see page 4 for symbol key).

BELOW: *The handsome evergreen,* Choisya ternata, *has a wonderful display of scented flowers in late spring.*

TOUGH SHRUBS

The shrubs in a garden form its basic framework. They are long-lived plants and, if they are to grow up alongside young children and family pets, will bear the brunt of energetic outdoor activities, and will need to be strong and sturdy to survive. The first year after planting is the most crucial, and they will need plenty of water to ensure quick establishment and good roots.

EVERGREEN SHRUBS

Mexican orange blossom (*Choisya ternata*) ◑ ✳

This handsome plant has glossy green leaves and gives a glorious display of scented white flowers in late spring. In very cold areas it needs the protection of a wall that faces the sun, but if frost damage does occur it will often rejuvenate well after pruning. It is quick-growing and does well in shade. Height and spread 2.5m (8ft).

Euonymous (*Euonymus fortunei* 'Emerald 'n' Gold') ◑ ❁

This is an excellent gold-variegated small shrub to brighten up dark corners. The leaves turn bronzy-pink in winter. Height and spread 1.5m (5ft).

Lavender (*Lavandula angustifolia* 'Hidcote') ○ ❁

This is the most compact lavender, with deep purple flowers. Keep it bushy by lightly trimming back after flowering, using a pair of shears. Height and spread 75cm (2½ft).

Rosemary (*Rosmarinus officinalis* 'Miss Jessop's Upright') ○ ✳ ❁

Being fast-growing and evergreen, with attractive flowers and wonderfully aromatic leaves that are ideal for cooking purposes, rosemary has all the qualities of a good garden plant. The common variety forms a rather wide, loose bush,

ABOVE: Sambucus *'Plumosa Aurea'*.

but 'Miss Jessop's Upright' has a more vertical habit and is altogether superior. Height and spread 2m (6ft).

Viburnum *(Viburnum tinus)* ● ✳ ✖

A large, fast-growing plant, this makes a good backdrop in almost any situation – even in deep shade. The flowers appear in late winter and are white with a sweet scent. 'Eve Price' is the most compact variety, and produces buds that are flushed with pink. Height and spread 3m (10ft).

DECIDUOUS SHRUBS

Berberis *(Berberis thunbergii* 'Erecta') ○ ✳ ✿ ✖

This densely branched, prickly shrub has a stiff vertical habit that contrasts well with more rounded shrubs. Although deciduous, it colours and fruits well. Height approximately 1.5m (5ft) and spread 45cm (18in).

Purple filbert *(Corylus maxima* 'Purpurea') ○ ✿

Few plants make such a strong impact as this one. It grows quickly, forming an erect bush with purplish buds and catkins in spring, and large, deep purple leaves all summer. Height 6m (20ft) and spread 5m (15ft).

Tree mallow *(Lavatera* 'Barnsley') ○ ✳

A vigorous bush with white flowers fading to pink, this plant flowers well in hot, sunny positions or in partial shade. It is a first-class plant for instant effect and sheer mass of flowers. Prune to within 15cm (6in) of the ground every spring to keep it compact. Height and spread 1.5m (5ft).

Rose *(Rosa glauca* syn. *R. rubrifolia)* ○ ✳ ✿

Robust and hardy, this excellent rose has attractive leaves, flowers and fruit. Greyish-purple young shoots and leaves are borne on delicately arching stems, followed by single, pink flowers and then bright red hips in autumn. Height 2m (6ft) and spread 1.5m (5ft).

Sambucus *(Sambucus racemosa* 'Plumosa Aurea') ◑ ✖

Golden-yellow, deeply cut, feathery leaves give this elder an airy appearance. Deep purples and blues show off the leaves and give a stunning contrast. Height and spread 3m (10ft).

Weigela *(Weigela* 'Bristol Ruby') ○ ◑

Large, deep-red, trumpet-like flowers are produced in early summer on branches weighed down with blossom. Prune after flowering by cutting back the shoots by about half. This plant is extremely hardy and grows well in sun or semi-shade. Height and spread 2m (6ft).

CLIMBERS AND WALL SHRUBS

Californian lilac *(Ceanothus 'Puget Blue')* ○ ✳
This is the toughest of all Californian lilacs, and has a dense mass of blue flowers in the spring. It does well when trained against a wall. Height and spread approximately 1.5m (5ft).

Flowering quince *(Chaenomeles speciosa)* ◑ ○ ✿
This is one of the few flowering shrubs suitable for training on to a wall that does not face the sun, and it has exotic, colourful flowers followed by golden-yellow autumn fruits. Although not the true quince, the ripe fruits make a delicious, tangy quince jelly. Height 1m (3ft) and spread 2m (6ft).

Clematis *(Clematis montana)* ◑
Most clematis species have very delicate and brittle stems that are easily broken, but this one is so vigorous that it soon clambers out of harm's way to settle on top of the nearest wall, creating a cascade of flowers in spring. Clematis is a

BELOW LEFT: Clematis montana.
BELOW RIGHT: Humulus lupulus.

ABOVE: Hydrangea petiolaris.

twining plant and needs wires or a trellis to twist around. The summer-flowering types such as C. 'Jackmanii' are suitable for small patio areas in a family garden. They should be pruned right to the ground every spring; the resulting soft, young stems are less brittle than those of the spring-flowering clematis varieties. Height and spread 7m (23ft).

Golden hop *(Humulus lupulus 'Aureus')* ● ◑ ○
This climbing plant dies down in winter, but makes up for this in the spring, when it is one of the first climbing plants to emerge, heading off up the wall or fence at an incredible rate. But you certainly will not begrudge this beautiful, golden-leaved, delicate plant any wall space, because it is a star performer in any garden. Height and spread 6m (20ft).

Climbing hydrangea *(Hydrangea petiolaris)* ◑ ○ ✖
Although the flowers of this species are not as showy as other hydrangeas, they make an attractive feature on this useful

and decorative plant. This is a true self-climber that clings to walls or fences by little root hairs growing out from the stems. It is valuable on a wall that receives little sun, where it will flourish. Although it is deciduous, in winter the tracery of the bare, reddish-brown, peeling stems makes an interesting feature. Height and spread 15m (50ft).

Honeysuckle *(Lonicera* x *americana)* ◑ ○ ✖
This magnificent, very free-flowering, vigorous climber has large, white, scented flowers that fade to yellow and produce a spectacular flowering display in early summer. It is excellent for covering ugly corners, and for scrambling up trellises and walls or over other bushes. Height and spread approximately 7m (23ft).

GROUND COVER
Ajuga *(Ajuga reptans* 'Burgundy Glow'*)* ● ◑ ○ ❀
This provides an evergreen carpet of plum-purple leaves, with upright spikes of blue flowers in early summer. Height 20cm (8in) and spread 45cm (18in).

Lady's mantle *(Alchemilla mollis)* ◑ ○ ❀
The soft, light green leaves of this plant make small mounds that erupt with frothy, lime-green sprays of flowers in early summer. It looks wonderful with roses. Height 30cm (12in) and spread 25cm (10in).

Siberian bugloss *(Brunnera macrophylla)* ◑ ❀
This grows and flowers quite happily in shade under leafy trees and shrubs. It has large, heart-shaped leaves that soon form dense clumps, and branching sprays of small, pale blue flowers that brighten up difficult situations. Height 45cm (18in) and spread 30cm (12in).

RIGHT: Vinca minor variegata.

Heuchera *(Heuchera micrantha diversifolia* 'Palace purple'*)* ◑ ❀
This plant has large, glossy, almost beetroot-red leaves that make dense clumps and contrast well with the sprays of tiny white flowers. Height and spread 30cm (12in).

Periwinkle *(Vinca major)* ● ◑
This ground-cover plant is more invasive than *Vinca minor*, but is useful for awkward corners in which little else will grow. Height 30cm (12in) and spread 1m(3ft).

Periwinkle *(Vinca minor)* ● ◑ ❀
This creates a dense, almost flat mat of glossy evergreen leaves and violet-blue flowers in summer. It is quick-growing and useful for dry, shady areas. Height 15cm (6in) and spread 1m (3ft).

BOUNDARY FEATURES

Good-looking boundaries that become a feature in their own right are particularly important in a small garden. They can add drama and height, while at the same time freeing the centre of the garden for play.

More than anything else, aspect influences the choice of plants. There are many options for the sheltered conditions of a sunny wall or fence, and there is a smaller, but valuable, selection of plants for a wall that faces away from the sun but is sheltered from frosts.

A wall that is exposed to sharp morning frosts provides the harshest conditions and the biggest challenge. This is a situation in which the many different varieties of ivy come into their own, creating interesting and effective backdrops with contrasting leaf shapes and colour. Ivy is easy to keep under control by pruning, and does no damage to a healthy wall. In fact, it can be argued that it keeps the wall dry and the house warm by providing a leafy covering that keeps off even the heaviest rain.

A few plants are truly self-climbing and can be left to negotiate a flat wall by themselves: for example, ivy and climbing hydrangea (*Hydrangea petiolaris*) use aerial roots to cling to the wall, whereas virginia creeper (*Parthenocissus quinquefolia*) has aerial sucker pads. Other climbers require a network of wires or trellising to which they can cling. Clematis has twining tendrils that lock tight as they dry, and wisteria has twining stems. Other plants that are not strictly climbers have to be tied to a support; climbing roses, ceanothus varieties and chaenomeles all fall into this category.

CLIMBERS AND WALL PLANTS FOR EVERY ASPECT
South and West
Ceanothus, Chimonanthus praecox, Choisya ternata, climbing roses, *Fremontodendron californicum, Lathyrus odoratus, Magnolia grandiflora, Wisteria sinensis.*

North
Camellia, Forsythia suspensa, Humulus lupulus 'Aureus', Hydrangea petiolaris, Lonicera, Parthenocissus.

North-east and East
Chaenomeles speciosa, Cotoneaster horizontalis, Hydrangea petiolaris, Jasminum nudiflorum, Kerria japonica.

TRELLISES
Trellis panels add another dimension to walls and fences, and sturdy versions make valuable free-standing screens. Invest in a quality product to use for supporting deciduous or herbaceous climbing plants, because it will be bare and visible for most of the year. A coat of coloured paint can

BELOW: *Canary creeper (*Tropaeolum peregrinum)*. This colourful creeper flowers from summer until the first frosts start.*